THE ARTS & CRAFTS

LIFESTYLE AND DESIGN

THE ARTS & CRAFTS
LIFESTYLE
AND DESIGN

WENDY HITCHMOUGH
PHOTOGRAPHS BY MARTIN CHARLES

Watson-Guptill Publications/New York

DEDICATION

For my parents, Geoff and Rosemary Hitchmough

Designed by David Fordham
Display type designed by Nina Barnett
Design copyright © Pavilion Books Limited

First published in the United States in 2000 by
Watson-Guptill Publications
a division of BPI Communications, Inc.
770 Broadway, New York, New York 10003

Library of Congress Catalogue Card Number : 00-103207
ISBN 0-8230-0314-0

First published in Great Britain in 2000 by
Pavilion Books Limited, London House, Great Eastern Wharf
Parkgate Road, London SW11 4NQ

Printed and bound in Singapore by Imago
First Printing, 2000
1 2 3 4 5 6 7 8/07 06 05 04 03 02 01 00

FRONT COVER: Dining room at Standen
BACK COVER: William Morris curtain and wallpaper at Standen
PAGE 1: Inglenook in the living hall at Blackwell, designed by M. H. Baillie Scott, 1898
PAGE 2: Hollybank, designed by C.F.A. Voysey in 1903
PAGE 3: Appliquéd hangings at Rodmarton Manor, designed by Hilda Benjamin (see page 125)

■ CONTENTS ■

CHAPTER ONE

PUTTING THE
ARTS & CRAFTS
HOME TOGETHER

LEFT: The hall fireplace at Standen,
designed by Philip Webb in 1891,
with ruby lusterware by William
De Morgan.

HE PURPOSE OF THIS BOOK is to consider the ways in which objects, interiors, and buildings were put together and used after they left the Arts and Crafts designer's studio. It examines the wider influence of the style and the way that Arts and Crafts products could be purchased from exhibitions, across the counters of department stores, or ordered from the pages of catalogs and magazines. Organized as a room-by-room guide to the home, it explains how the decoration and furnishing of different rooms were specifically tailored to enhance domestic ceremonies and to create settings for social behavior. Complete interiors by progressive designers are compared with the rulings of etiquette manuals and household directories of the period so that their shock value in bending or breaking codes of conduct can be allied to their aesthetic innovations. By establishing the social context for Arts and Crafts designs and by describing the ways in which furniture, fabrics, wall-coverings, light fittings, and ornamental features were brought together to create room settings, the book identifies the connections between different kinds of objects and reinstates the client as an animating presence. Without patrons and customers Arts and Crafts barely would have got off the drawing board. Its houses and their contents were designed, primarily, to be used.

The role of objects and patterns in the home has barely been touched upon in studies of Arts and Crafts. The way that houses were lived in and the separate functions and decorative customs of each of the rooms were fundamentally important, however, to issues of design at the turn of the century. Strict rules of propriety and good taste governed who did what in each of the rooms and an almost universally accepted system of conventions dictated precisely how a dining room, a bedroom, or a kitchen was furnished and arranged. Textiles and furniture which have become museum pieces and collectors' items, too precious for everyday use, served as accents or props in the daily rituals of domestic life. An Ashbee piano, for example, was designed to be unfolded and played in the drawing room or the living hall by the light of its own integral candles in the evenings. Its compact, square form challenged the prevailing belief that ordinary upright pianos were common and bourgeois and the use of ornament in unassuming inlays around the exterior of the case, opening to reveal images of flowers in richly colored enamels, alluded to the public reserve and more private passions of young women who learned to play the piano in order to perform for romantic suitors and to entertain their families.

The organization and decoration of the Arts and Crafts home were standardized to a remarkable extent and every conceivable situation was anticipated and addressed by codes of correct behavior. The hero in Edith Wharton's *The Age of Innocence* despaired at the conformity and predictable conditions which threatened to map his entire life: "We're all as like each other as those dolls cut out of the same folded paper. We're like patterns stencilled on a wall."[1] Only the "artistic" were permitted to break the mold without incurring a reputation for vulgarity, but uniformity, if it was questioned at all, was welcomed as a liberation in most instances. In one of the most authoritative and thorough assessments of the English house, written in 1904, Hermann Muthesius concluded that the English derived their confidence and easy assurance from a tyrannical system of rules and customs which dictated what people must wear and how they must behave, and that this determined the furnishing and arrangement of their surroundings. It was never necessary for them to worry about formalities—about where to put the display cabinet, for example, or which room would be most auspicious for a proposal of marriage—because these matters were ruled by strict social conventions.

"The most striking characteristic that the foreigner notices about the English is that their patterns of life are immutable and fixed for all time. . .Not only is the domestic routine in the individual house unvarying and as punctual as clockwork throughout the

LEFT AND RIGHT: The "Manxman" design introduced a contemporary accent to Arts and Crafts pianos. The compact folding case, which closed like a cabinet around the keyboard when it was not in use, was particularly convenient in smaller Arts and Crafts homes but there was a sexual symbolism, too, about the plain exterior which only revealed its decorative riches and beauty when it was opened for play. This fine example was designed by C. R. Ashbee in 1903.

year but all households of similar economic standing are as like one another as peas in a pod. So one can classify the households of England according to income and know at once precisely how things will be done in a household of a given class. They have the same number of servants and the work is apportioned in exactly the same way, they have the same rooms, the same meals, the same daily routine."[2] Muthesius's account of domestic design is corroborated by a plethora of published and private material from the period including diaries, biographies, drawings, photographs, novels, and magazine articles by diverse sources. Although the conventions which he describes seem obsessive to readers today, they were so habitual to everyday life in early twentieth-century England that the fact that they called for explanation would have seemed curious a century ago.

The decoration of each room and the objects with which it was furnished responded precisely to the status of its occupants and the uses to which it would be put. The Arts and Crafts hall was invariably furnished with a sturdy table, set to one side, where the outdoor clothes of visitors were laid—with hat and gloves on top and umbrella or walking stick to one side. To place such a table among the more delicate furniture of the drawing room would have been unimaginable. Equally, no sink was provided in the English Arts and Crafts kitchen and it would have been a gross lapse to have installed one because washing up and the preparation of vegetables were always relegated to a kitchen maid in her separate scullery. A strict understanding that no self-respecting housewife would ever cross the threshold to the kitchen was reflected in the styling and materials that defined the room as a functional work space. In a typical Voysey house, the family areas were furnished with oak-paneled doors and molded baseboards, but the kitchen was fitted with painted pine doors of a battened-and-ledged cottage style and the baseboards were plain and square-cut. Even the proportions of the baseboards indicated the status of the room: they were an inch lower in the kitchen than those in the rest of the house.[3] This systematic classification of materials and decoration to define the functions of the different rooms was not invented by the Arts and Crafts Movement. It formed part of a cultural legacy founded in aristocratic traditions which the Arts and Crafts Movement rationalized or usurped.

The planning and decoration of American country houses perpetuated British traditions, not least because the domestic routines and social conventions they were designed to accommodate conformed, with only subtle variations, to European standards. In the novels of Henry James, Americans are often stylishly defiant of Old World traditions. American Arts and Crafts houses were more daring and inventive than their British counterparts, but even in the deliberate breaking of bonds they consciously made reference to the aristocratic traditions of a European heritage. The Arts and Crafts Movement in Britain and America was concerned with reform, however, and with the ideal of the simple life as a means of reevaluating existing traditions and returning to a rational foundation. They wanted design and decoration to break away from outmoded and nonsensical conventions and adhere, instead, to a system of meaning and integrity which was pertinent to the lives of its clients and their designers.

The reputations of a few key designers have been analyzed in detail in previous studies of Arts and Crafts, and the development of a coherent style can be traced

LEFT AND ABOVE: Art glass by Emil Lange (left) was used throughout the Gamble House in lanterns, cupboard doors, and as iridescent glazed passage doors, and windows between interior spaces so that the jewel-like accents of the interiors altered with the daylight. In the tree-of-life front door, viewed here from the interior (above), creative design and technical mastery were combined with an inspired manipulation of natural light.

through the philosophies and the pioneering designs of such figures as Morris, Webb, Stickley, and Greene and Greene. The importance of the movement has been assessed with comparable usefulness through specialist studies of particular crafts. The Arts and Crafts Movement achieved extraordinary standards in the design and execution of architecture, furniture, ceramics, textiles, and the arts of fine printing and bookbinding. Previously published discussions of the similarities and differences between Tiffany art glass, for example, and that of Emil Lange highlight common influences and the chemical advances that enabled glass to be tinted and layered to create new iridescent effects at the turn of the century. They say very little, however, about the different ways in which art glass was used in the domestic interior; we believe this issue of context and consumption is crucial to a rounded understanding of the work.

The requirements for a stained-glass panel in a front door, designed to be viewed from both sides, are different from those for a lamp shade, for example. Aside from variations in scale, which photographic reproductions negate, the appearance of a glass panel that is naturally illuminated will alter through the course of a day. The tree-of-life triptych, designed by Charles Greene and executed by Lange to fill the front door of the

Gamble House in Pasadena, California, bathes the entire hall in a golden light when the sun shines through it early in the morning. The leadwork is on the exterior so that it reads as a skeleton, defining the structure of the tree to visitors arriving at the house during the day. At night, when its colors are artificially lit by the interior, it acts as a luminous focus of the darkened exterior of the house. The Tiffany table lamp which ornaments the Gamble House drawing room, in contrast, depends for its effect on a consistent artificial light source which is either on or off. Because it is an electric lamp, it was associated with modernity while the stained-glass triptych of the door recalls ecclesiastical traditions. The door's tree-of-life design has a spiritual significance in the visual language of Arts and Crafts, and the California oak trees which inspired the design contribute an acute sense of place. The butterfly motif on the lamp has a lighter, more incidental decorative value as a conversation piece in a room which was devoted to the niceties of entertaining.

Arts and Crafts is narrowly defined as a movement in architecture and design history which began with the design of the Red House for William Morris in 1859 and ended with the outbreak of the First World War. Its origins can be located in the British Gothic Revival designs of A.W.N. Pugin and the parsonages of William Butterfield, which embodied the modest restraint and the reverence for local materials and building techniques which later Arts and Crafts architects took as their foundation. In the 1870s and '80s the idea of the "house beautiful" crystallized around a reevaluation of ordinary domestic objects; a veneration for blue-and-white china and exquisitely simple white and palest gray interiors gathered momentum. Historians have rooted this earnest taste for simplicity and for the stylized, reductive elements of Japanese design in the Aesthetic Movement, but there were no rigid divisions between Arts and Crafts and Aesthetic ideals in the nineteenth century. Both movements were summarized by William Morris's famous aphorism, "Have nothing in your houses that you do not know to be useful or believe to be beautiful," which Oscar Wilde adapted for his lecture tour of America in 1882.[4]

Artists and critics instigated the idea that the decoration and furnishing of the home should be a creative endeavor. Their conviction that ostentatious decoration was insincere as well as vulgar and that some materials were more "honest" than others introduced a moral agenda to issues of style. The determination among artists and designers that every detail of the house and its arrangement—from the handle on the front door to the cupboards in the butler's pantry—should be scrutinized and redesigned to conform to a vision of the house as a work of art, was evenly matched by market forces. The stream of books, lectures, and articles which they supplied on every dimension of home decoration was eagerly taken up by consumer demand, as Clarence Cook noted in *The House Beautiful*, published in 1881. "There never was a time when so many books written for the purpose of bringing the subject of architecture. . .down to the level of the popular understanding, were produced as in this time of ours."[5]

The Arts and Crafts period coincided with a building boom in Britain and America. Homeownership became achievable for the first time for a growing number of unskilled

ABOVE: Frank Lloyd Wright, "A Small House with 'Lots of Room in It,'" published in *The Ladies' Home Journal* in 1901.

and semiskilled workers, and the ideal of a second home in the country became a reality for the more affluent middle classes. The influence of progressive and fashionable designers inevitably filtered down to the more derivative detailing of speculatively built houses and the styling of furniture manufactured in batches for department stores. The Arts and Crafts Movement is distinguished, however, by the active participation of its leading protagonists in promoting better design at every level of production. Frank Lloyd Wright, Gustav Stickley, C.F.A. Voysey, M. H. Baillie Scott, and Parker and Unwin all devised plans and elevations for economical small houses and "picturesque cottages." For a dollar or so, architects in America, working independently or for property developers, would send brochures of their domestic designs to prospective clients and for as little as five dollars a complete set of plans, elevations, and details could be purchased mail-order and erected by a local carpenter. The transition from a ready-made design to an individual commission was easily achieved. One investment company selling building plots for bungalows offered "to incorporate your ideas into any of the hundreds of plans we have on file, or we will draw new plans" for a small additional fee.[6] For more limited incomes, the "ready-cut" house provided the cheapest form of home with Arts and Crafts potential. Prefabricated in a factory, it arrived on the back of a freight car in a set of numbered boxes. Manufacturers boasted that a skilled carpenter could assemble one of these timber-frame houses in a day but the inexperienced bridegroom took a little longer, as Buster Keaton demonstrated with disastrous consequences in the silent movie *One Week* (1920).

Designs for Arts and Crafts homes were advertised and promoted in popular American magazines like *The Ladies' Home Journal*, which published plans and perspectives by Wright for "A Home in a Prairie Town" and "A Small House with 'Lots of Room in It'" in 1901. More specialized publications, like Stickley's *The Craftsman*, first published in 1901, made a direct connection between the selection of a mail-order design for a new home and the marketing of Arts and Crafts furniture and fittings to put in it. Subscribers to the Craftsman Home-Builders' Club, founded in 1903, were offered plans, elevations, and specifications for every kind of house including bungalows, farmhouses, and country cottages. *The Craftsman*'s authoritative articles on decoration, handicraft, and needlework were published "to meet the specific demands of its subscribers." Colored perspectives of complete interiors, together with detail illustrations of furniture and fittings, enabled them to mix home-crafted pieces with Stickley products purchased from the Craftsman Workshop and its franchises.[7]

American Arts and Crafts evolved independently from its British counterpart. There was a dialogue between the two movements and in style and philosophy they were compatible, drawing on the same sources. There were significant differences, however, even in the way that texts by John Ruskin and William Morris were interpreted by their British and American followers. While the British Arts and Crafts Movement was burdened by a harrowing sense of responsibility for the social consequences of industrialization and a profound commitment to the preservation of ancient buildings and traditions, industry was regarded as a civilizing influence in America. As generators of wealth and power, the scale and inventiveness of industrial expansion in America

"The Craftsman House"   Designed by E. G. W. Dietrich

LEFT: Drawings, watercolors, and photographs of buildings and their interiors had a currency as influential images at the turn of the century quite distinct from the reality of the buildings. This perspective was published in *The Craftsman* in 1903.

RIGHT: James MacLaren, cottages at Fortingall in Perthshire, c.1889–90.

were sources of national pride and cultural identity. The ideal of the simple life, of wholesome cottages and rural crafts, regarded with nostalgia in Britain, was connected in the American consciousness with the pioneers. Frontier settlements were recent history, less than a century old in most of the cities where Arts and Crafts took hold. In fact, the international exposition marking the centenary of American independence, held in Philadelphia in 1876, is often quoted as the starting point for Arts and Crafts in America.[8]

The trail blazing confidence and imagination that founded vast commercial empires in the United States was combined with a more conservative attitude toward the arts. Classical buildings were erected in stone, according to European conventions, as monuments to wealth and power. The evolution of a distinct American culture in architecture and design materialized through the American Arts and Crafts Movement gradually and tentatively. In Britain, Arts and Crafts was known in the 1890s and early 1900s as the Modern Movement (not to be confused with that of the 1920s and '30s), and its appeal for American clients and designers lay in a culturally loaded combination of tradition and innovation. Paris was perceived as the artistic center of Europe throughout the nineteenth century and most American architects trained at the Ecole des Beaux Arts. The image of the English country house touched an ancestral nerve in American domestic architecture, however, and perspectives of Olde English designs with half-timbered gables were lavishly illustrated in the architectural journals of the period.[9] For many American clients and designers who could trace their ancestors back to European origins within two or three generations, the culture of Europe formed part of their sense of personal identity and heritage.

English Arts and Crafts architects and designers studied the forms and decorative simplicity of traditional cottages and farmhouses as examples of domestic design refined through centuries of use. Unsullied by the artificial constructions of style and the application of preposterous ornament that plagued Victorian design, they were reformed and adapted to meet the rational demands of a modern age. This juxtaposition between the image of Olde English traditions as a reassuring and often sentimental connection with the past and as the basis for progressive change coexisted in America with the Classical tradition of the Beaux Arts. Images of buildings and complete interiors by British designers were widely circulated through books, exhibitions, and magazine articles, but their most profound influence was felt in the houses which looked least like English country houses.

American architects such as Charles and Henry Greene, Bernard Maybeck, and Frank Lloyd Wright translated the philosophy rather than the more obvious superficial attributes of English Arts and Crafts into an American idiom. The Arts and Crafts conviction that a house must belong to a place and its people, and that it should be built of local materials using time-honored methods passed down through generations of builders, presented American designers and their clients with a directive for innovation. The dramatic extremes of climate and topography and the cultural diversity among the people and building types that characterized the different states of America suggested very different architectural models and design solutions than the English cottage and manor house. Spanish missions, crude adobe huts, and the rough redwood cabins of early settlers were as pertinent to an American culture of colonization as the formal English country house plan imported by more affluent immigrants. The American Arts and Crafts Movement was motivated, in part, by a determination to assert its cultural independence from Europe. Its clients and designers were conscious, nevertheless, of a complex continuing relationship with the British movement and its origins.

Issues of preservation were inseparable from the origins and evolution of English Arts and Crafts. Historic buildings, whether they were crumbling medieval churches or redundant farm buildings, were charged with a sharp social significance. Their fragility as cultural relics, as evidence of ancient crafts and communities during a century of sweeping changes, accrued an emotive value. When the Society for the Protection of Ancient Buildings was formed in 1877, its founding members included painters, writers, and Arts and Crafts clients, as well as architects. William Morris and Philip Webb were the originators of the society, which shared Morris's reverence for ancient buildings as precious heirlooms. Morris's vision of a society capable of honoring "the little grey, weather-beaten building, built by ignorant men, torn by violent ones, patched by blunderers, that has outlived so many hopes and fears of mankind and yet looks friendly and familiar to them" was fundamental to a perception of architecture as an inspiration to culture and community.[10] His ideal of building as the embodiment of human aspirations was one of the founding principles of the Arts and Crafts Movement.

For Webb, too, buildings were living things, a revelation of humanity. He regarded their destruction as akin to murder: "You see, it's my grandmother," he would say of a building in danger of demolition.[11] The scholarly and physical understanding of traditional building methods and materials that enabled him to advise on the conservation and repair of buildings for the society at weekly meetings, which took place above Morris & Co.'s Oxford Street showroom, became "a real school of practical building" for a younger generation of Arts and Crafts architects. The architectural

ABOVE: Cottages at Fortingall by the
Scottish architect James MacLaren
romanticized the picturesque
qualities of rural building traditions.

LEFT: "The Vision" by George Frampton, one of the many sculptors of the Art Workers' Guild.

RIGHT: The St. Agnes tapestry (right), first produced by Morris & Co. in 1887, exemplifies the Arts and Crafts principles of fellowship and collaboration. The figure was drawn from a stained-glass design by Burne-Jones while the flowers and fruiting tree were by Morris. Morris & Co. tapestries, William De Morgan ceramics (left), and bas-relief sculpture including Frampton's "The Vision" were all exhibited and offered for sale by the Arts and Crafts Exhibition Society in London.

nucleus of the society was supported by a committee which included the philosophers Thomas Carlyle and John Ruskin; the author of the *National Biography* and father of Virginia Woolf, Leslie Stephen; and the painters Sir Lawrence Alma-Tadema, William Holman Hunt, and Sir Edward Burne-Jones.

Painters and sculptors were as important to the early direction of the English Arts and Crafts Movement as the architects, designers, and craft workers with whom they joined forces in the formation of the Art Workers' Guild in 1884.[12] They were more sophisticated than their designer colleagues in the use of symbols to convey meaning in a work of art. They also understood the potential of the independent exhibition as a vehicle for the avant-garde, a means through which artists could declare an affinity with one another and communicate directly with critics and the public at large. The Impressionist exhibitions of 1874 were followed with interest by British painters, and their own dissatisfaction with the Royal Academy and its hierarchies provided a common incentive for establishing the Art Workers' Guild. A knowledge of the practicalities of organizing exhibitions, however, and the double risk of financial disaster and professional humiliation, made these painters counsel caution when their architect colleagues proposed a public exhibition at the guild's inaugural meeting, and for the first four years of its existence, the guild confined itself to private meetings.

Structured somewhere between a masonic lodge and a gentleman's club, the Art Workers' Guild excluded women from its membership. It was committed to "Unity of the Arts" and to an ideal of brotherhood "as a real, living and inspiring motive in our arts and crafts and also in our lives."[13] Specialist papers were read at its monthly meetings and small exhibitions and demonstrations described innovations and traditions in technical processes such as lacquerwork, embroidery, and wood engraving. An insistence on "absolute privacy" prevented the substance of its learned discussions from reaching a wider public, however, and it was not until 1888, when the Arts and Crafts Exhibition Society was founded, that the principles of Arts and Crafts, nurtured and refined within the guild, were made public.

If the Art Workers' Guild provided Arts and Crafts with a social forum and a dynamic professional focus, the first Arts and Crafts Exhibition gave the movement a coherent public identity. The term "Arts and Crafts" was initially coined as a name for the Exhibition Society by the bookbinder T. J. Cobden-Sanderson. It was adopted in America nearly a decade later when the first American Arts and Crafts exhibition was held in Boston in April 1897. The Boston and Chicago Arts and Crafts societies were founded in the same year. Although in London the Exhibition Society was an offshoot of the Art Workers' Guild, the exhibitions were organized on an open basis, providing women and amateurs as well as professionals in every field of the decorative arts and crafts with an opportunity to show their work. The exhibitions were designed to engage with the public, to promote a more critical appreciation of the arts in everyday use, and to inspire a revival of arts and crafts as a means of creative expression in the home. Because the exhibitions were initially intended as annual events, they also generated new work. In addition, a series of evening lectures and presentations, including a "Tapestry and Carpet Weaving" demonstration by Morris, explained the processes of craftsmanship, introducing the guild's specialist style of discussions to the public at large. This pioneering program of events acted as a catalyst in the production of Arts and Crafts. But it was equally influential in identifying and cultivating an Arts and Crafts clientele.

These events offered the public an opportunity to buy—and by showing completed commissions they inspired more enlightened patronage. Stained glass and mosaics designed for public buildings provided dramatic accents and gave makers an opportunity to show their most ambitious work, but the elementary stages of patronage were encouraged as well as its boldest gestures. At many of the smaller exhibits, items such as ceramics and jewelry were offered for sale and purchasers were encouraged to deal directly with the makers, laying the foundation for further commissions. The exhibitions were held at a progressive London gallery, accentuating the claims of the exhibits as works of art and providing a favorable context for the high prices attached to them. The lectures and demonstrations explained the costly and laborious processes of craftsmanship. They appealed to the cultural aspirations of the middle classes and, for those unable to visit in person, popular magazines like *The House* and *Homes and Gardens* described the highlights of the exhibitions as design trends which could be adapted and incorporated into the ordinary home. At the same time, specialist periodicals like *The Studio* focused on the creative development and originality of individual artists.

Alongside photographs and drawings of their most recent buildings, architects showed actual chimneypieces and furniture destined for their clients' new houses. No serious attempt was made to assemble the work into room settings, however, until the 1902 International Exposition at Turin presented the idea of the interior as a complete work of art. Department stores like Liberty and Heal's displayed their products and the services of their interior designers in showpiece rooms beginning in the 1890s and, although sales were an important aspect of the Arts and Crafts Exhibitions, comparisons with commercial enterprises were consciously avoided. The appeal of a table lamp or a wallpaper as a consumable was secondary to its importance as an example of good design and fine craftsmanship.

There is a misconception that the Arts and Crafts Movement rejected machine production absolutely. Approved industrialists like the wallpaper manufacturers Jeffrey & Co. were given their own stand in the London exhibitions and their Arts and Crafts credentials—the presence of some of the most eminent artists of the day among their designers—were accentuated at the expense of the more mundane issues of price and availability. The fact that these same artists all served on the Exhibition Society's selection committee may have influenced the prominence of Jeffrey & Co.'s position in

ABOVE: Complete interiors were lavishly illustrated in magazines and catalogs. This drawing room was designed by Liberty & Co. and published in *The Studio Yearbook* in 1907.

the exhibition, particularly as their own status as designers rested, in part, on the artistic integrity as well as the commercial success of industrialists who mass-produced their patterns. Nevertheless, there was a genuine determination to support manufacturers who promoted artistic design: in the 1893 exhibition the skilled processes involved in making wallpaper were emphasized by demonstrations of block and roller cutting alongside a display of Jeffrey & Co. blocks for the successive stages of wallpaper printing.

Attitudes toward mass production were mixed within the Arts and Crafts Movement. The degradation of the factory worker, reduced to a mechanical role by the processes of industrialization, was vehemently criticized. Pugin's *Contrasts* (1836), Carlyle's *Past and Present* (1843), and Ruskin's chapter on "The Nature of Gothic" in *The Stones of Venice*

(1851), presented moral and aesthetic arguments for a return to traditional methods of production. Morris defended hand craftsmanship as a political issue, claiming it as the art of the people, a vital expression of "their sense of the beauty and mystery of life" which was imperiled by capitalist brutality.[14] These assertions were revered and variously interpreted by artists and designers in Britain and America later in the century, but they were equally influential in creating a receptive market for the products of Arts and Crafts.

Innocent tastes for fancy souvenirs and cheaply decorated but shoddily made factory goods were condemned by Ruskin and his followers as culpable weaknesses in some of the most vitriolic attacks ever leveled against consumers. Ruskin denounced machine-made ornament when it was a convincing imitation of handwork as a lie: "It is an imposition, an impertinence, and a sin."[15] Cast-iron decoration was "so cold, clumsy and vulgar," he wrote, that it was incapable of masquerading for the fine lines and surface textures of wrought and hammered work. He reviled it as evidence of a depraved, self-indulgent taste. His moral recriminations were restyled into sardonic observations by Oscar Wilde, who told an American audience in 1882 that the "funeral urns" with which iron stoves were commonly embellished were "as great a bore as a wet day or any other particularly dreadful institution."[16]

Wilde was not earnest enough to be eligible as an Arts and Crafts pioneer, although many of his maxims would qualify. He claimed that his mission as an aesthetic leader was inspired by an encounter with Ruskin when he was an impressionable undergraduate in Oxford. He and his friends were persuaded to build a road between two villages "for the sake of a noble ideal." After two months of breaking stones and wheeling barrows along planks ("a very difficult thing to do"), in the rain and mud of an Oxford winter with Ruskin working at their side, the elder critic left for Venice, and the road building came to an abrupt end in the middle of a swamp.[17] For Wilde, the abandoned road was a tale of inspired endeavor. He made no comment on the ludicrous prospects of a troop of privileged undergraduates posturing as laborers, but the anecdote highlights a common flaw in the philosophy of Arts and Crafts. By requisitioning an ideal of the simple life and its "honest" forms of labor, Ruskin and Wilde engaged in a masquerade, a sophisticated form of role-playing which was fundamentally dishonest. Their assumption that the rudimentary processes of road building were easily assimilated was an affront to the strength and skill of the laborers they mimicked, and the unfinished road dealt the local community a double insult. Wilde's anecdote, like the self-styled apprenticeships by Arts and Crafts architects (for half a day or half an hour) to craftsmen whose lives had been devoted to perpetuating traditional techniques, illustrates a patronizing disrespect for practical experience.

Although there were purists in England and America for whom Arts and Crafts represented an unconditional rejection of industrial methods, who established their workshops in rural communities and revitalized traditional techniques through the creation of unique objects, they were a minority. Their example served as an ideal for clients as well as their fellow artists and designers. For most of their contemporaries, however, the economic opportunity of machine production to extend the market for

artistically designed and well-made products was accepted as a social and technological challenge. Wilde described the inherent beauty and grace of the machine and extolled its importance in the service of modern production: "We reverence it when it does its proper work, when it relieves man from ignoble and soulless labour, not when it seeks to do that which is valuable only when wrought by the hands and hearts of men."[18]

The early Arts and Crafts exhibitions were motivated by a practical determination to redefine the role of art and craftsmanship within the manufacturing industry and in the workshops that supplied many of the large firms of decorators and furnishers. According to Walter Crane, one of the Exhibition Society's most proactive members, the exhibitions were a revolt against "that so-called industrial progress which produces shoddy wares, the cheapness of which is paid for by the lives of their producers and the degradation of their users." They represented more of a reformation than a revolution, proposing realistic solutions to some of the problems that faced manufacturers. The anonymity of industrial production and the dilemma of manufacturers, "forced to make their appeal to the unreal and impersonal average, rather than to the real and personal you and me" in order to secure a profitable share of the market, was answered by a resolution that the individuality of the "impersonal artist or craftsman" should be reinstated.[19]

Arts and Crafts designers were celebrated as influential personalities whose opinions as well as individual styles would be of interest to the general public; this was part of a deliberate strategy to raise architecture and the decorative arts to the status of painting and sculpture. The Arts and Crafts Exhibition Society in London stipulated that the names of the designers and makers of all the pieces exhibited, whether independent artists or employees, must be published in the catalog. While the advantage of a discriminating public, capable of recognizing the work of leading designers, was self-evident, the society's rules were regarded with suspicion by many large stores and manufacturers: "Several of them refused point blank to have anything to do with a scheme under which the work of art should have any name attached to it except that of the proprietor and vendor."[20] The suggestion that employees should enjoy a separate recognition outside the workshop was a deliberate threat to management hierarchies.

The Arts and Crafts Movement was inextricably linked with political and romantic attitudes to socialism. While the arts of painting, sculpture, and embroidery were associated with aristocratic refinement and dilettante talents, the decorative arts and handicrafts were connected with trade and a lower social order. Artistic claims for unity paralleled political demands for equality. The open organization of the Arts and Crafts Exhibitions presented a model for democratic cooperation. Politically sensitive pieces were shown in the form of embroidered banners, and the exhibitions were

LEFT: W.A.S. Benson was one of the many independent designers who supplied the Morris & Co. showroom with affordable and artistically designed products.

regarded in some quarters as a rallying point, a creative union for art workers isolated in workshops across the country. However, the movement's political potency was confounded by disparate ideologies and deliberate ambiguities.[21] William Morris, the movement's most influential socialist, dismissed the "militant socialism" ascribed to Cobden-Sanderson's mandate that all designers and makers be named: "It was not by printing lists of names in a catalogue that the status of the workman could be raised, or the system of capitalistic commerce altered in the slightest degree."[22]

While Morris's philosophy as a socialist influenced the ideals and working practices of his more committed followers, his position as a successful businessman generated a fashion for Arts and Crafts which ultimately made the style affordable and accessible to a vast market. He combined an innovative practice, creating original and extravagant interiors on commission, with the production of affordable mass-produced fabrics, wallpapers, and simple batch-produced furniture. Morris & Co. devised hand-painted and uniquely fashioned interiors for such prestigious addresses as St. James's Palace. Less affluent clients, completing new country houses or revamping old ones, were content with the company's personal interior decorating service, which created Morris interiors from the firm's own range of patterns and furnishings. By the 1880s, Morris & Co. could offer "Painted Glass; Embroidery. . .Arras tapestry; Hammersmith carpets; Axminster, Wilton and Kidderminster carpets. . .Printed cloths for wall-hanging, curtains etc; Wallpapers," and less renowned designers were specifying products and complete interiors from their line. Householders who could not afford the services of an interior decorator could buy Morris fabrics and wallpapers by the yard or the roll, or select single items—a De Morgan vase or a Sussex chair—from their catalog or their Oxford Street shop. The firm's products were designed as components to be assembled into room settings so that they could be tailored to serve the most modest demands. It was this unilateral appeal, the adaptability of Morris's style to satisfy aristocratic tastes for costly materials and meticulous workmanship, as well as a more popular demand for light, pretty patterns, that underpinned his success and that of the Arts and Crafts Movement as a whole.

A review of the Oxford Street shop noted "the spirit of individuality and unity. . .we do not see a variety of conceptions in different styles, nor a number of patterns by various artists; all the work is exceptionally good, and is due to Mr. Morris himself we believe."[23] Morris did not design the company's complete line. Philip Webb was responsible for many of the three-dimensional products including candlesticks, glassware, and furniture. It was Morris's creative determination which persuaded the best artists and designers of the period to work independently or collaboratively for the company. However, it was his energy and commitment, combined with effective marketing, that established a taste for the pared-down simplicity, relieved by a few well-chosen and imaginatively displayed pieces, that was the essence of Arts and Crafts.

The Arts and Crafts Movement was concerned with social as well as aesthetic reform. Ruskin's conviction that architecture and design had an affect on the character of an individual ("All architecture proposes an effect on the human mind, not merely a service to the human frame") persuaded philanthropists and designers to provide Arts and Crafts dwellings for the working classes—whether they wanted them or not.[24] A model sitting room for a "Workman's Small House" designed by Morris for a Manchester philanthropist was exhibited in the city's new art gallery in Queen's Park in 1884, accentuating the importance of artistic design in everyday objects. The furniture and fittings, including Morris's "Daisy" wallpaper, light fittings by W.A.S. Benson, and a Lethaby washstand, would have been beyond the means of most workmen, and the prestigious Manchester department store that supplied them would not have welcomed new customers in hobnailed boots, even if they had chosen to brave their way past the doormen.[25] The room and its trappings were part of an idealized image of cottage simplicity conjured up by Arts and Crafts designers for the middle classes, but the lines of influence ran in two directions. Ascetic Arts and Crafts clients who wanted to emulate the living conditions of the rural poor were outnumbered by the aspiring middle classes, whose social ambitions were flattered by the notion that the rich interiors illustrated in magazines like *The Studio* could be replicated in their own front parlors, boasting the same designers' names at a fraction of the cost.

Books and magazines about fashion and style in the home proliferated during the Arts and Crafts period. Pitched at the newly "respectable" middle classes, they promised essential guidance for readers who could not depend upon their mothers or the services of an interior designer for sound advice. They were complemented by encyclopedic volumes on household management (Mrs. Beeton's first tome was published in 1861) and etiquette manuals which prescribed the correct dress and behavior for any given situation. Together these volumes present a stupendously detailed account of how life was lived in the Arts and Crafts home. Books of a similar kind tend to borrow from their predecessors, but the information in late nineteenth-century novels and biographies, in art periodicals, popular magazines, household manuals, and guides to "manners and social usages" corroborate one another to a remarkable extent.

Fluid connections between fine-art criticism and popular culture are exemplified in the manuals and magazines that guided the consumer toward "the house beautiful." Many of the early style books, including Charles Eastlake's *Hints on Household Taste* (published in England in 1868 and in America four years later) and Clarence Cook's *The House Beautiful* (published in New York in 1877), were written by art critics. A periodical for artists and designers, *The Studio* (launched in 1893), created a critical forum for Arts and Crafts, but its lavish articles, interviews, and exhibition reviews also created celebrities. In fact, the designer label was invented by *The Studio*: in 1896, after three years of conscientiously promoting the same names, it was able to claim that "Now a 'Voysey Wall-paper' sounds as familiar as a 'Morris chintz' or a 'Liberty silk.'"[26] *The Studio* was widely read by influential Arts and Crafts collectors as well as practitioners throughout Europe and America, generating an elite international market for the products of Arts and Crafts. In 1901 it was joined by *The Craftsman* magazine, which effectively defined and coordinated the Arts and Crafts Movement in America.

Both of these magazines operated at the serious end of Arts and Crafts. They gave voice to the philosophies behind the objects. They promoted the ideal of unity in the arts and in the home, the rational basis for simplicity, and the reverence for nature and natural materials that gave the movement an art historical integrity. The first issue of *The Craftsman* opened with lengthy appraisals of Morris and Ruskin, paying homage to the British origins of the movement and establishing a distinguished provenance for American developments. The importance of Morris as a founding father and an enduring inspiration was reiterated in *The Studio* as well as *The Craftsman* well into the twentieth century. While *The Studio* was concerned with the products of Arts and Crafts as works of art, however, *The Craftsman* set out to articulate and popularize a coherent American style of architecture, interior design, and furnishing which could be adapted to ordinary needs. As publisher of the magazine, Stickley generated a market for his own products through the illustrations and editorial content of *The Craftsman*, nurturing and educating a taste for shingled houses with interiors decorated and furnished entirely in the Arts and Crafts style.

Magazines belong to the culture of consumption. They present architecture and interiors as objects of desire, as designer settings for lifestyles to which their readers might aspire. The watercolor perspectives of complete interiors in *The Studio* and *The Craftsman* shaped the identities of those magazines and served as tokens of style and affluence to be displayed, ever so casually, in design-conscious living rooms. The same images acquired a fashionable currency through circulation in magazines that enhanced their commercial value. An element of gloss attached itself to the reputations of architects who were featured in *Country Life* and *Homes and Gardens* and an object

ABOVE: Interior perspectives such as this bedroom, published in *The Craftsman* in 1905, were designed to inspire ordinary householders as well as the owners of Craftsman homes.

purchased from an Arts and Crafts Exhibition singled out for special attention in a *Studio* review acquired a particular cachet.

Arts and Crafts was the first design movement to consciously negotiate a place for itself in popular culture. Its practitioners were determined, almost from the outset, to communicate with the masses as well as the classes.[27] In addition to *The Studio* and *The Craftsman*, which maintained an informed editorial commitment to Arts and Crafts, its appeal as a fashionable style assured it a place in less specialized magazines like *The House Beautiful* and *The House* (both launched in 1897). These cheaper magazines set out the practical ramifications of the style, mixing Arts and Crafts with other fashionable styles of the period. They translated the most progressive design initiatives into a form that was attractive and accessible to the general reader, suggesting ways in which existing interiors could be modernized and adapted to Arts and Crafts. Although *The House* occasionally bent the rules, sacrificing the finer points of craftsmanship and "making do" in the interests of economy, it offers a significant insight into the ways in which ordinary people and their homes were affected by the movement.

The idea of the woman as homemaker was enshrined by the Arts and Crafts Movement. The concept that it was demeaning for a woman of means to take paid employment coincided with increases in homeownership and unprecedented levels of literacy, a consequence of compulsory education. Magazines and books about the home were written for (and often by) women with leisure and money at their disposal, so that issues of style and decoration were feminized. A regular feature in *The House* combined the pleasures of shopping with the creation of fashionable interiors. "In Search of 'the Latest'" scoured manufacturers' catalogs, specialist shops, and department stores for affordable and well-designed products. Sound-bites of artistic philosophy were mixed in a chatty formula with the names and addresses of manufacturers. A new range of bedsteads by Heal's, for example, was recommended for its hygienic properties, while illustrations of table linen designed by Walter Crane and Lewis Day were accompanied by a statement from Day that, "A well-ordered table appeals first to the eye, next to the sense of smell, and then to the palate."[28]

The house was regarded as an extension of the feminine body, and the furniture and fabrics with which it was decorated were a continuation of more personal statements in dress and jewelry. "There are now dozens of journals which have to do with the dressing and adornment of the body; but, strange to say, there is not one dealing exclusively or specially with the dressing of the house."[29] At a time when articles in women's magazines were increasingly open to strident feminist demands and women writers were claiming their rights to political and intellectual equality, *The House* presented its readers with a world of creative opportunities within their homes. It validated the traditional work of women by focusing on the domestic environment and it amplified women's creative role in stitching and assembling their own clothes, for example, by urging them to apply their "frail fingers" to the crafting of copper finger plates and repoussé mirror frames. This amateur work, whether or not it culminated in professional recognition, was the bedrock of Arts and Crafts as a participatory movement. Its appeal, however, and the change it dictated in the domestic status of women, from household managers to creative stylists, was double-edged.

The House kept women in their place, diverting their energies away from politically more effective (but aesthetically less appealing) activities. In a period when dress reflected the individuality, social status, and moral correctness of the wearer, as well as an ability to follow fashion, the potential for failure in "dressing" the house with adequate care or taste carried with it the threat of personal recriminations. Although it was conspiratorial in matters of taste, *The House* was typical of household manuals of the period, such as Cassell's *Book of the Household* (1869–71) and H. C. Davidson's *The Book of the Home* (1904), in its imperious tone, which played on the insecurities of new homeowners. In the first issue it promised its readers, "We shall take possession, and peer and poke into every corner of the domicile, from the kitchen to the roof assuming, indeed, the role of a friendly

RIGHT: The drawing-room bay at Standen was designed for intimate conversations and needlework. No window was provided in the west-facing wall so that the bay never became too warm on summer afternoons.

critic to the family."[30] An Arts and Crafts obsession with cleanliness was reflected in articles which rooted out the unhealthy and unhygienic. Nailed-down carpets that couldn't be taken outside for cleaning were condemned as "receptacles for all kinds of dust and dirt," and even wallpapers and paints were suspected of harboring unseen perils.[31] The responsible housewife was instructed to test them for poisonous pigments.

Complaints by women that the home had become a "quiet, unnoticed whirlpool that sucks down youth and beauty and enthusiasm" were ignored.[32] Charlotte Perkins Gilman's reasoned appeal for a form of communal living that would liberate women from repetitive domestic duties was not included in the Arts and Crafts canon. She articulated a perpetual dilemma, nevertheless, and although her use of language is characteristic of Arts and Crafts, the frustrations she describes are as relevant for women today as they were for her contemporaries nearly a century ago. "Life is complicated, duties conflict, we fly and fall like tethered birds, and our new powers beat against old restrictions like ships in dock, fast moored, yet with all sail set and steam up."[33]

As clients, as homemakers, and as professional art workers, women were presented with mixed messages by the Arts and Crafts Movement. Ruskin insisted that "the woman's true place and power" must be in the home. "She must be enduringly, incorruptibly good; instinctively, infallibly wise—wise, not for self-development, but for self-renunciation; wise, not that she may set herself above her husband, but that she may never fail from his side; wise, not with the narrowness of insolent and loveless pride, but with the passionate gentleness of an infinitely variable, because infinitely applicable, modesty of service—the true changefulness of woman."[34] In the decades around the turn of the century, the changing expectations of women, often contradicting or renegotiating this patriarchal and essentially Victorian attitude, were among the most dynamic factors in reforming the planning and decoration of the Arts and Crafts home. Underlying tensions between masculine and feminine definitions of what the home should be and how it should respond to changing lifestyles were as fundamental to the evolution of Arts and Crafts as the more openly discussed reconciliation between tradition and innovation.

The styling of the home, the choice of papers, fabrics, and furniture were regarded, traditionally, as the responsibility of the mistress of the house. Just as the different rooms were designed for different purposes, they were designated masculine or feminine and decorated accordingly. The dining room was a masculine space, where the hierarchy of the family and its servants was clearly articulated by the seating and serving arrangements around the table. It was the room where ancestral portraits were hung, where the family congregated for mealtime rituals, and the decoration of the room was invariably somber and traditional. The living room, by comparison, was the feminine domain where guests were entertained to afternoon tea and the family and its close friends were invited to withdraw after dinner. Whereas the dining room was planned around a central focus— the laid table—the living room was designed to accommodate the disparate social groupings of informal parties. Every detail of the room, from the arrangement of the furniture in intimate clusters to the placing of small rugs on the floor, and the use of wall sconces and table lamps to define these separate groupings, contributed to an impression of informality and delicacy. The Arts and Crafts architect who prescribed every detail of the interior stymied some of the creative autonomy enjoyed by late Victorian women in the design and decoration of their homes. In most instances, however, there was a creative collaboration between the woman as client and her designer.[35]

The innovations in design that distinguish Arts and Crafts houses from their Victorian predecessors often accommodated or negotiated a degree of propriety for unconventional domestic arrangements. In an age when women were learning to play billiards and to smoke as demonstrations of modernity, and when many patrons were keen to disassociate themselves from their ancestral roots, domestic customs were called into question. A Victorian insistence upon segregating the sexes at every opportunity and, in larger houses, on the provision of separate rooms for different activities was revoked. The free-flowing spaces in Arts and Crafts houses and the subtlety with which the decorative languages of masculine and feminine spaces communicated with one another responded to changes in use and to progressive attitudes toward the consumption as well as the production of Arts and Crafts designs. Respectability, however, demanded at least a semblance of conformity to traditional codes of behavior. There was a thin line—as Henry James demonstrated in his novels *Daisy Miller* and *The Awkward Age*—between an innocent, even fashionable disregard for formalities and behavior which would inevitably result in ostracism.

The Arts and Crafts home framed the attitudes as well as the activities of its occupants. It was reassuringly traditional and disconcertingly modern by turns, confounding expectations by decorating the billiard room with a pretty, feminine paper or by building bookshelves into the drawing room where, in conservative circles, serious subjects were considered unsuitable. There were fundamental rules, laid down over generations, which Arts and Crafts clients and their designers could only bend. However, objects and interior designs, whether they challenged or accentuated domestic traditions, belonged to a complex system of references and regulations that governed the planning and decoration of every room in the house. The full significance of Arts and Crafts designs, the ways in which they were shocking or amusing to consumers at the turn of the century, can only be understood within this context.

In Britain and America alternative systems of value were resurrected and romanticized to legitimize change. The ideal of the simple life and of the medieval household, each with its own impeccable provenance, debunked the extravagant materialism and hierarchical structures which had riddled Victorian culture and design. They cast a mist of nostalgia around radical innovations. They existed as compatible, parallel systems, however, which could be embraced wholeheartedly or adopted piecemeal as remedies for outmoded conventions which were contrary to the demands of modern living. The principle of unity, that every detail of the home down to the silver teapot should contribute to a harmonious totality, is widely acknowledged as an edict of Arts and Crafts. The idea that objects related to the dress and jewelry of the people who used them, and that they were designed to dignify a domestic ceremony or to accentuate a particular aspect of an interior, belongs to an older tradition, however, which the Arts and Crafts Movement underscored.

CHAPTER TWO

THE BUILDING AS BODY

LEFT: Kelmscott Manor in Gloucestershire was more than the Morris family's country retreat. For Morris, the Elizabethan manor was a building of iconic significance.

 HEN HE WAS FIRST INVITED into the dining room of William Morris's Kelmscott House in Hammersmith, a borough of Greater London, in the 1880s, playwright George Bernard Shaw wrote that he was instantly and deeply affected. "I saw at once that there was an extraordinary discrimination at work in this magical house. Nothing in it was there because it was interesting or quaint or rare or hereditary, like grandmother's or uncle's portrait. Everything that was necessary was clean and handsome: everything else was beautiful and beautifully presented. There was an oriental carpet so lovely that it would have been a sin to walk on it; consequently it was not on the floor but on the wall and half way across the ceiling. There was no grand piano: such a horror would have been impossible. On the supper table there was no table cloth: a thing common enough now among people who see that a table should be itself an ornament and not a clothes horse, but then an innovation so staggering that it cost years of domestic conflict to introduce it."[1]

Kelmscott House was not designed like an Arts and Crafts building as Morris's country house in Kent, the Red House, had been. Nor could it claim the Elizabethan provenance of Kelmscott Manor in Gloucestershire, which Morris believed had

33

"grown up out of the soil and the lives of them that lived in it." It was a Georgian town house fronting the Thames River. Damp and neglected when Morris found it in 1879, it had already been rejected by the painter Dante Gabriel Rossetti, who described the stairs to the basement kitchen as "a sort of ladder with no light at all, in which smashes would I think assail the ear whenever a meal was going on."[2] Morris negotiated a reduction in the rent, offering only £85 per year when a comparable house in good decorative order would have cost half as much again. He spent nearly £1,000 on redecorating it, however; the equivalent of a year's salary for a comfortably off member of the middle classes. The blood-red flock wallpaper and the long black painted bookcases of the previous occupants were stripped away, and the house was refurbished with Morris & Co. fabrics and papers using the "extraordinary discrimination" which Shaw later praised.

An accomplished poet, designer, and businessman, Morris was typical of successful entrepreneurs and professionals of his era in that he could afford a place in the country as well as a town house. As a young man he had commissioned his friend Philip Webb to design a complete house, Red House in Kent, for himself and his new bride. However, he had retained his bachelor rooms in London: it was there in Red Lion Square that he established the firm of Morris & Co. in 1861. When Morris had to give up Red House in 1865 because his private income diminished, the firm moved to a Georgian house in Queen Square, Bloomsbury, with workshops, offices, and showrooms on the ground floor and accommodation for the Morris family on the floors above. As Morris & Co. expanded, opening a separate shop on Oxford Street in 1877, the family moved to the town house in Hammersmith and their apartments were given up to the firm.

Kelmscott House was named after Kelmscott Manor, which the family used as a weekend retreat from 1871. Unlike the Red House, both the London town houses and the Gloucestershire manor were rented. Architecturally they were very different in style and layout, but in their decoration they can all be classified as Arts and Crafts. The Red House provided the movement with an architectural manifesto; Morris's other houses were more representative of the housing options which were generally available to Arts and Crafts consumers. They describe an evolution of Arts and Crafts interiors, irrespective of building type, which matured more than a decade before the architectural masterpieces for which the movement is renowned were designed (in the 1890s and early 1900s).

However, the importance of the Red House has overshadowed the significance of Morris's subsequent homes. Within fifty years of its completion Muthesius touted it as "the first private house of the new artistic culture, the first house to be conceived and built as a unified whole inside and out, the very first example in the history of the modern house."[3] It was through the furnishing and fitting of Red House, he claimed, that Morris "discovered his true mission in life" as a decorator. In the family's apartments in Queen Square and their Hammersmith and Gloucestershire homes, Morris was obliged to work within existing structures. The architectural ideal which

ABOVE: The Red House, designed for Morris by his friend Philip Webb, and proclaimed in 1904 as the very first modern house.

Muthesius and other architects and critics later regarded as a fundamental element of Arts and Crafts—that the plan of the building and its decoration should be conceived as a single coherent statement—was not applicable. It was a situation which Morris shared with many of his own clients and with the majority of Arts and Crafts consumers, and it was his ability to shape the tenets of Arts and Crafts around an existing structure which made his London houses so influential.

The family rooms in Queen Square provided Morris & Co. with an opportunity to present privileged customers insight into how their wallpapers and fabrics could be used in a domestic setting. Morris flouted the convention that "no self-respecting family lives

in a house that has a shop below it" and joked that he "lived over his shop."[4] Boundaries between the artist and the customer were disregarded at Queen Square. Interested visitors to the showrooms were invited into the basement to see experiments in the dyeing vats. Or they might be introduced to the stained-glass painters at work in a long corridor leading to an old ballroom at the rear of the house. There, tables were covered with "the jewel-like colours of the glass. . .and the silvery net-work of the leading." May Morris recalled that her father brought his work into the family rooms: "In the evenings—what delight! there sometimes appeared a gloriously, mysteriously shining object, behind which he would work with bright cutting tools on a little block of wood, which sat on a plump leather cushion."[5] He was cutting the woodblocks for Burne-Jones's illustrations to *The Earthly Paradise*.

Morris's customers as well as his friends were occasionally entertained in the "noble" drawing room. The finest room in the house, with five windows looking out over the square, it was "made to shine with whitewash and white paint" and decorated with Morris & Co. wall hangings. On special occasions dinners were held in this room, and the long oak table was laid with blue china and delicate green glasses designed by Philip Webb and made by James Powell & Sons for the firm. May Morris described them gleaming "like air-bubbles in the quiet candle-light" and reflecting in little mirrors set into the chimneypiece. Her nursery, high up at the top of the house, was hung with "Trellis," the first wallpaper Morris ever designed, but she recalled with some amusement that in spite of his reputation as a fine designer of wallpaper, he regarded wallpaper as "a makeshift." "Red House. . .had no papers: the walls were hung with embroideries, or painted with patterns by himself and pictures by the friends. None of the living-rooms at the Manor where I write are papered; those that are not panelled or tapestried are hung with chintzes. So a country house should be furnished with material easily removed for cleaning—or just white-washed."[6] Tapestries, she concluded, were for the "well-to-do" while "humbler folk" were satisfied with paint.

The idea that work and domestic life were inseparable was fundamental to Morris's philosophy. The liberties which he took with the different rooms of the house as a consequence, however, using the drawing room for special dinners and for work, were highly irregular. When the family first moved to Hammersmith a loom was set up in Morris's bedroom so that he could rise early every morning and begin the day with a period of weaving. The stables were furnished with massive hand-looms and the first hand-knotted Hammersmith rugs were marked with a distinctive hammer and a blue zigzag to symbolize the river setting where they were woven. Whenever a big carpet came off the beams the family was summoned across the garden to admire it before it was sent to the Oxford Street shop and on one occasion, when an exceptionally high tide flooded the stables, the entire household and its guests rushed to the loom room to rescue a vast carpet destined for Naworth Castle.[7] The stables and coach house were converted into a hall for socialist meetings after Morris became involved in politics. Although it remained the family home until after Morris's death in 1896, and it became the heart of an Arts and Crafts enclave, Kelmscott House was never fundamental to Morris in the way that his sense of history and community were anchored in Kelmscott Manor. May Morris recalled: "I do not think he ever felt in his heart that the house he named Kelmscott House was our real home; it was a convenient and seemly shelter from the weather, a place to keep books and pretty things in, but at best a temporary abode. . .No house in London could ever be invested with the passionate delight he had in our dear riverside home, the home of his dreams, with its poet's garden."[8]

In Britain, unlike the rest of Europe, the town house was a necessary compromise: "No one doubts for a single moment that city-dwelling can never be more than a mere makeshift, an enforced substitute for the ideal of the freehold, free standing country-house."[9] The appeal of landownership and the ideal of the country house were inseparable from the fact that, historically, all land reverted to the Crown. Half of England, in 1904, was still owned by only 150 landlords, and Britain was the only country in the world in which the principal royal residence was not in the capital. Every well-to-do family, from the aristocracy downward, enjoyed or aspired to a place in the country with a smaller residence in town. The country seat, whether a hereditary home or a place that was rented for the summer, was the focus of family life.

The country house was the setting for social events, for courtships, and business deals, and it was equipped with guest bedrooms and service wings that could cater to a substantial number of guests. The character Lady Geraldine in Shaw's novel, *Love Among the Artists*, reclaimed the management of her house and dairy farm after a season's absence just in time to marry one of her guests off to a wealthy industrialist and to welcome a director of the Electro-motor Company, brought home from work by her husband, as "a pioneer of the invading army of autumn visitors." She complained that "a couple of electro-motors" would soon be harnessed to the pony carriage and that she had become weary of the task of entertaining the legion of businessmen and politicians whom her husband invited to wind down for a fortnight at their Devonshire home. "So they run

ABOVE: The Homestead, designed by
Voysey in 1905–6, epitomized the
cottage ideal as a country retreat that
was simple and compact but
artistically detailed and crafted.

down," she quipped, "and it is seldom by any means possible to wind them up for
conversational purposes until they go away again." [10]

Aristocratic traditions were so firmly rooted in the British cultural consciousness that
they filtered down to the most modest and the most progressive country houses. When
C.F.A. Voysey designed The Homestead, a retreat at a seaside resort, for a successful
young insurance broker, the house was provided with five bedrooms and a full-sized
billiard table even though the client was a bachelor. An article in *The House* urging its
readers to invest £400 to £500 to build a cottage consciously evoked the ideal of the
hereditary estate, passed down through generations, as a motive: "You hope... that

perhaps one of your own family may be content to live in the same house after you. . .
may taste a little of the feeling of the old country families who for generations live in the
old manor house."[11] The Arts and Crafts period coincided with an agricultural recession
in Britain which released freehold land in the country: the old landed gentry found it
more profitable to sell tracts of land for building plots at the edges of their estates than
to farm it. In addition, new forms of transportation in Europe and America made the
rural retreat and the logistics of spending the weekend in the country increasingly
appealing. While economic growth transformed remote villages into popular resorts and
created fashionable new suburbs, however, the soaring commercial value of urban land
restricted housing options in the inner cities.

The rented house was socially acceptable and relatively common in nineteenth-
century England. In many cities a few immensely wealthy individuals and corporations
controlled the landholding, and in older cities like London entire districts were laid out
as leasehold properties so that "the landlord was showered with riches fleeced from the
population" every time the terms of his ninety-nine-year leases ended and the land could
be redeveloped.[12] Urban tenants were often restricted to a narrow choice of apartments
and houses, refined by generations of speculative builders to a few classic types designed
to provide the most efficient and elegant interiors for the minimum building cost.
Because these Georgian and Victorian buildings were standardized in plan and
elevation, and tenants were generally prohibited from making structural alterations, the
decoration of their interiors became a vital expression of individuality.

Relatively grand houses could be had quite cheaply as the expiry date for their leases
approached, promoting a broad social mix living in close proximity. The young Edwin
Lutyens, anxious to find a house worthy of his aristocratic bride-to-be (her mother was
a lady-in-waiting to Queen Victoria), was able to secure a four-story Georgian house in
Bloomsbury Square in 1897, formerly the offices of architect R. Norman Shaw, for a rent
of only £190 per year. "Although it looks grim and square outside, inside it is a paradise
. . .hardly a dark corner anywhere and all is fair, square, and spacious, with any amount
of cupboards and housewife's delights."[13] Lutyens's offices, like those of Morris & Co.
a short distance away, were arranged on the ground floor of the house but, where the
drawing rooms in each of Morris's houses created settings for his wife, the famous Pre-
Raphaelite model Jane Morris, it is more difficult to imagine the delicate, conventional
prettiness of Emily Lutyens at home in the striking professional statement of the
Lutyens's drawing room. The walls were painted black, contrasting against white
woodwork and yellow curtains, and the room was sparsely furnished with a red lacquer
cabinet and a black lacquer screen. The sofa was banished.

Morris's house in Hammersmith and Lutyens's Bloomsbury home presented
conventional elevations to the street. Typical of many turn-of-the-century town houses,
their exteriors conformed, demonstrating architectural good manners, to the
characteristics of the neighborhood, which meant the experience of surprise, on
entering the private interiors, was accentuated. Similarly, the layout of the British town
house was standardized. Muthesius observed that the basic form and organization of the

English terraced house had remained unchanged for 150 years. Tall houses with narrow street frontages maximized the development potential of the land. The kitchen and servants' quarters were relegated to the basement or a narrow annex at the rear of the house, with a separate entrance for tradesmen and deliveries. Storage cellars often extended under the pavement and in large houses the butler, as the most senior servant responsible for running the entire house smoothly, would have his bedroom at the front of the basement adjoining a burglar-proof plate room so that even in his sleep he could guard the family silver. In smaller houses the domestic quarters were limited to a kitchen equipped with larders and a pantry, and a separate scullery to the rear with a lavatory at the very back of the house for the servants' use.

The library, as a place of work or study, was at the front of the ground floor close to the life of the street outside. (The dining room was more secluded, located to the rear of the house within convenient distance of the kitchen.) From his study at Kelmscott House, writing his lectures and poetry, Morris would watch the ragged children from the neighboring slum who included the scrubbed steps to his front door in their play area. May Morris recalled that he would wait until he could endure their noise no longer and then he would "go out and beg them to give him a little peace and quiet and play elsewhere for a while."[14]

The drawing room—elevated above street level and literally resting on the library, the place of business, on the floor below—was invariably the finest room in the house. Its position on the first floor, overlooking the street and yet set apart from it, was emblematic of the status of the mistress of the house. While the man was recognized as the head of the household the woman, according to late Victorian culture, was at the center of its internal management and its identity as a home. "The social side of life is entirely in her hands, she keeps an eye on all exchanges with the outer world, issues invitations and receives and entertains guests. The man of the house, who is assumed to be engrossed in his daily work, is himself to some extent her guest when at home. So the drawing-room, the mistress's throne-room, is the rallying-point of the whole life of the house, the room in which one talks, reads and spends idle hours, the room in which the occupants assemble before meals and amuse themselves afterwards with conversation and play."[15] In spite of its importance as a meeting place for eminent painters, writers, and critics, Shaw described the drawing room at Kelmscott House as a temple to Jane Morris, whom he perceived as a silent, iconic figure: "When she came into the room in her strangely beautiful garments, looking at least eight feet high, the effect was as if she had walked out of an Egyptian tomb at Luxor."[16]

While the principal bedrooms were arranged on the second floor of the town house, a guest bedroom with its own dressing room and a bathroom were often provided on the first floor. Where a nursery was required it was situated on the third floor, with servants' accommodation in the garret at the top of the house. The segregation of the servants' quarters from the family rooms was welcomed for the privacy that it afforded both parties, but there were few delusions about the relative comfort and convenience of the servants' bedrooms high up under the roof. They were hot in summer and cold in winter and the servicing of the entire house with coal fires, hot water, and meals and refreshments all brought up from the basement kitchen was arduous and impractical. Even in the most modern and luxurious houses, equipped with running hot water, central heating, and "speaking tubes," as well as food and service lifts connecting the kitchen to the upper floors, the "tiresome servant-question" was one of the most effective incentives for reform in the design of the Arts and Crafts home.

In the 1870s and 1880s servants were easy to hire and they stayed year after year, often continuing as family retainers into their old age. Basement kitchens, steep secondary staircases, and the necessity of carrying water up three flights of stairs to bathe the numerous children in the nursery were a poor alternative, however, to the shorter working hours and higher wages offered by the shops, offices, and factories which flourished in the late nineteenth century. Householders who would not stoop to stealing servants from their friends (considered a worse offense than the stealing of a husband) were obliged to manage with smaller domestic staffs and to maximize their efficiency. Flats were promoted as a modern alternative to the "great squandering of energy" wasted in the passageways, lobbies, and stairs of the vertical town house. They were popular in both Europe and America, and from the 1880s mansion flats became increasingly fashionable in London. Easily shut down when they were not in use, they were recommended as the perfect adjunct to the country house and as stylish dwellings in desirable neighborhoods for small families, bachelors, and single women. More important than their economy and convenience, however, was the advantage that apartments required fewer servants.

The idea of the building as a body, in which each part was allocated a set place according to its function, resulted in a uniform regularity in the city, where houses were built speculatively and occupied by a succession of tenants. In the country house, where rooms could be spread out in different configurations rather than stacked one on top of the other, Arts and Crafts clients and their architects were free to relax the upright, formal conventions of orthodox appearances. The form of the building, its use of materials and its relation to the site could be more expressive. Arts and Crafts designers were experimental in their planning and they believed that the harmony and internal order of the house should be expressed in its architectural exterior. Nevertheless, they were bound by domestic customs and standard expectations, so that the organization of the country house, like its counterpart in the town, conformed to innumerable practical and cultural conditions which every client took for granted and every architect was required to learn as an integral part of his training.

Architecture and decoration, like the elaborate dress codes of the period, were governed by protocol and good manners. The Arts and Crafts Movement was peppered with idiosyncratic details which, like a flamboyant tie or a brilliant pair of socks, were designed to attract attention and contradict the implicit messages of an otherwise polite and discreet appearance. The planning innovations that extended the contours of the house into the garden and transformed the hall into a living room were compatible with dress reforms that encouraged fashionable women to abandon their crinolines and stays in favor of loose, flowing Pre-Raphaelite gowns. Arts and Crafts attracted a reforming generation of clients who depended upon the creative originality of their designers to clothe their progressive attitudes and lifestyles in a form which was modern and forthright, while making all the necessary references and concessions to good form.

Standen in West Sussex exemplifies the balance—on the part of both clients and architect—between tradition and innovation which distinguished the Arts and Crafts country house from its Victorian predecessors. The clients, James and Margaret Beale, were nonconformists with a taste for honest simplicity and good workmanship. James Beale was the son of a wealthy family of Birmingham solicitors who had made their fortunes as legal advisors to the Midland Railway. He had guided the railway company through a complex succession of parliamentary bills and legal negotiations which eventually secured the necessary permissions to build their London terminus, St. Pancras Station. As a consequence, Beale enjoyed a professional reputation for ruthless tenacity but he was typical, too, of a "new industrial aristocracy" of clients. They extended the commercial drive and rigorous standards of inquiry at the cutting edge of private enterprise to rationalize the organization of their private lives.

Commercial success was allied to a philanthropic sense of duty and public service in the Beale family. James Beale's younger brother was Lord Mayor of Birmingham, chairman of the city's Music Festival, and the first vice-chancellor of Birmingham University. As patrons, their taste in the arts tended toward subjects and styles which were readily understandable and relevant to contemporary values. Pre-Raphaelite paintings, the poetry of Tennyson, and Elgar's compositions, celebrated and romanticized English cultural traditions and portrayed a timeless pastoral counterbalance to modern urban life. They believed this art usurped the supremacy of Classicism, which they saw as an imported, academic culture that had been synonymous with aristocratic taste for generations.

The spectacular rural setting, the architectural references to time-honored building traditions, and the emphasis on solid materials and fine craftsmanship at Standen embodied the enduring fundamentals of Englishness for the Beale family and their architect, Philip Webb. These elements incorporated the preoccupations with nationalism and heritage which underpinned the Arts and Crafts Movement. Beale's father had invested his capital in a country estate and in doing so he had emulated the aristocracy. Although Standen was set on a substantial property, James Beale in the 1890s was typical of his generation in seeking to distill and revise the essential ideal of the country house into a modern retreat. The idea of the resplendent Victorian mansion burgeoning with elaborate architectural details and littered with a confusion of furniture was dismissed on aesthetic grounds by Arts and Crafts practitioners. For their patrons the army of servants and the failing agricultural returns associated with running such an extravagant establishment were pertinent disincentives.

A modest country house, streamlined to maximize the advantages of country life, Standen was characteristic of the Arts and Crafts Movement. It was conceived as a setting for relaxed family holidays, a convenient distance by steam train from the Beales' London home in the fashionable Holland Park district. The journey signified an emotional as well as a physical detachment from urban life. At the village of Oxted the fast train carrying

LEFT: The entrance court, Standen.

ABOVE: Garden elevation, Standen, designed by Philip Webb in 1891.

commuters from London was exchanged for "a little train on a siding that slowly chuffed through lovely country" and the last few miles along narrow country lanes were traveled in a horse-drawn carriage.[17] Earlier in the nineteenth century it had been necessary for successful entrepreneurs to relinquish all their ties with the commercial world before they were accepted by the landed gentry. However, James Beale, like many of his contemporaries, combined his business commitments in the city with weekends in the country. Margaret and their seven children spent longer holidays at Standen. They were dispatched with a proportion of the family servants and vast quantities of luggage for several months at a time. Luckily, the informal and imaginative planning of Webb's design catered specifically to the individual needs of the family and their domestic staff.

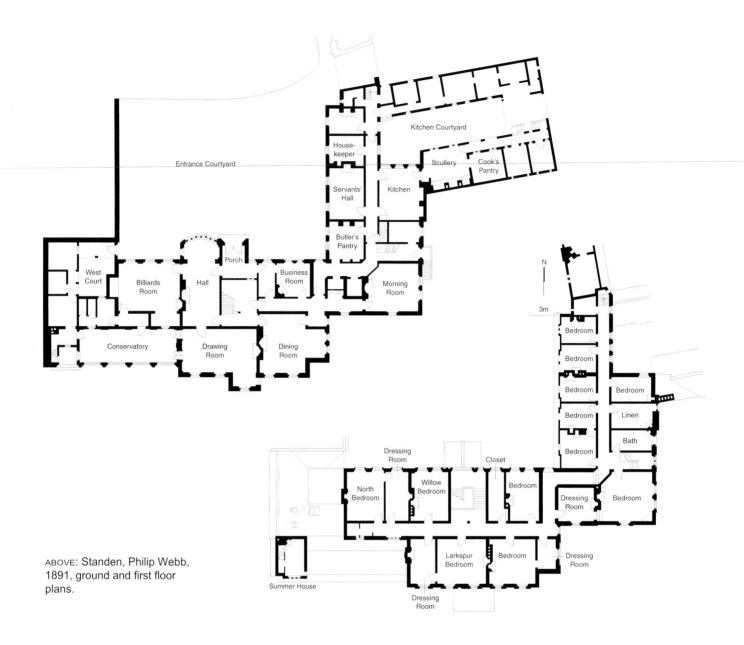

Entrance Courtyard

Kitchen Courtyard

House-keeper

Servants' Hall

Kitchen

Scullery

Cook's Pantry

Butler's Pantry

West Court

Billiards Room

Hall

Porch

Business Room

Morning Room

Conservatory

Drawing Room

Dining Room

N

3m

Bedroom

Bedroom

Bedroom

Bedroom

Bedroom

Bedroom

Linen

Bath

Dressing Room

Closet

North Bedroom

Willow Bedroom

Bedroom

Bedroom

Dressing Room

Bedroom

Larkspur Bedroom

Bedroom

Dressing Room

Summer House

Dressing Room

ABOVE: Standen, Philip Webb, 1891, ground and first floor plans.

Margaret and James Beale's grandchildren remember arriving for holidays at Standen as a sequence of sensations. Their carriage from the station delivered them into an enclosed courtyard in front of the house and as they stepped into the porch they were assailed by "the special Standen aroma of dried rose petals, eucalyptus and mimosa." [18] Webb provided a generous porch and cloak room where drafts could be contained and outdoor clothes removed. The family accommodation was arranged in a rectangular block with the principal rooms overlooking the garden on the south side and a separate service wing at right angles, framing the east side of the entrance court. James Beale's "business room" was tactically positioned between the two on the north side of the house, overlooking the entrance and buffered by the adjacent cloakroom from the noise and distractions of the main family rooms.

Beyond the entrance porch, Webb provided a substantial hall, paneled and furnished as a living room with a wide fireplace around which the family and its friends could gather for afternoon tea and musical recitals. The "living hall" was an Arts and Crafts invention, popularized by Webb and founded on a romantic notion of the medieval hall in which a larger social family, comprised of servants and estate workers as well as the gentry, would congregate to eat, drink, and sleep.[19] In smaller Arts and Crafts cottages and bungalows almost the entire ground floor was planned as a multi-purpose "living hall" in a practical determination to sweep away the conventional warren of tiny rooms. In larger houses like Standen, however, the hall was a subtle subversion of Victorian values. There, the traditional masculine and feminine spaces of billiard room and drawing room both opened directly onto the hall. By providing a neutral, third reception room at a time when attitudes toward chaperoning and appropriate behavior for young women were in a state of flux, Webb undermined the moral zeal of earlier Victorian country houses.

RIGHT: The living hall, where the Beale family congregated for musical recitals and afternoon tea, was originally painted red as a prelude to the light, south-facing drawing room.

BELOW: The entrance porch at Standen was generously planned with a cloakroom to one side.

LEFT: The billiard room at Standen doubled as a library. Webb designed a raised seating alcove with a perfect view of the table and in 1898 he added a second, more intimate bay to the corner of the room.

RIGHT: The drawing-room bay at Standen was furnished with built-in window seats, forming an intimate space for reading and needlework within the room.

Further concessions to a quiet revolution in lifestyle were made in the billiard room itself. Traditionally this was an exclusively masculine domain where the men of the house would retire after dinner to smoke and drink. It often had its own separate entrance "by which visitors may [could] enter in the evening and leave, possibly late at night, without coming into contact with the rest of the household."[20] By the late nineteenth century, however, progressive young men were less prone to regular bouts of heavy drinking and progressive young women were inclined to join them in a cigarette and a game of billiards.[21] At Standen, the billiard room was used as a smoking room in the mornings but it also served as a family library, chipping a second notch out of the traditionally male Victorian preserve. In 1898 the original seating area, raised in its own bay at the end of the room for spectators, was augmented by a pretty alcove tucked into the corner of the room. Papered with Morris's Pomegranate design, it was an inglenook for gossip and intimacies, designed to accommodate only the most peripheral interest in a view of the table.

Margaret Beale was a gifted seamstress and a keen gardener. Her drawing room was given the most prominent position on the south side of the house. To maximize the daylight for needlework, Webb projected a deep bay into the garden with windows on two sides. His Gothic training and his acute sensitivity to the English climate were too deeply instilled, however, to permit French windows or a semiglazed door opening directly onto the terrace. The Arts and Crafts Movement pioneered the idea of the garden as an extension of the house, divided into a series of "outdoor rooms," each with its own separate character, arranged to complement the plan of the interior. Margaret Beale was typical of a generation of women who became practical gardeners.[22] Many of her contemporaries were inspired by the example of Gertrude Jekyll, who wrote about gardening as a traditional craft and whose own borders were arranged and planted as works of art. The garden at Standen, however, was more likely to have been influenced by the Beales' distinguished neighbor, William Robinson, who initiated the natural style of planting that complemented the formal garden plans designed by Arts and Crafts architects.[23]

Margaret Beale's gardening diary describes her expertise as a plantswoman, and her passion for gardening was contagious. On wet afternoons when the lawn was too soggy for tennis her daughter Helen organized the family in obsessive pruning and cutting-back expeditions, leaving mountains of debris for the gardeners to clear away the next morning. Because Standen was designed primarily for use in summer, the garden and its lawns for tennis, bowls, and croquet were central to the interests of the family. It was a creative space for Margaret Beale and her artist friends. Her London neighbor Aglaia Coronio, who modeled for Rossetti and flirted with Morris, sent her sketches for suggested trellis designs after an afternoon at Standen. However, in spite of the garden's

RIGHT: Conservatories are rare in Arts and Crafts houses. At Standen the stifling humidity of the Victorian conservatory was supplanted by an airy circulation space where the codes of conduct dictated by each of the interiors were relaxed.

importance to the life of Standen, Webb retained a formal division between the house and its garden.[24] His followers would have drawn an axis southward through the hall and drawing room, leading out through a veranda into a garden path which might have terminated in an arbor or a summer house. Instead Webb created an axis leading westward from the drawing room into a long conservatory with a door in the end wall, which in turn led into a staircase vestibule. Steps downward opened into a sheltered recess with a garden seat partially enclosed by the walls of the house, but the narrow staircase also led up to a summer house raised above the terrace. This was the room that Webb promised as a small-scale commission to Helen Beale when the seven-year-old child asked him to build "a Little Room specially for her." He charged her a penny for the design.[25]

Conservatories are rare in Arts and Crafts houses because these spaces were associated with the artificial hothouse conditions of Victorian horticulture rather than the natural abundance of indigenous plants that characterized the new style of gardening. In Webb's country house plans, however, rooms opened directly into one another so that corridors were only used where they were needed to articulate the circulation of the house and to separate spaces. At Standen a conservatory connects the billiard room with the drawing room; the architectural language of the space, with rendered walls and iron girders supporting a glazed roof, differentiate it from the refined decoration of the surrounding interiors. In Victorian novels, events which contravene the niceties of polite behavior take place in the garden. Its connotations with wild nature and its detachment from the regulated social behavior conditioned by the different interiors of the house made it an ideal setting for romantic propositions and daring revelations or confrontations. At Standen the conservatory serves as an intermediary space between masculine and feminine rooms, between the artificial order of the interiors and the law of nature beyond. It contributes to a subtle layering of spaces which reflected a relaxation in the domestic rituals of Victorian country life while maintaining an air of propriety and social ease.

Every evening the Beales dressed for dinner and congregated in the drawing room until James and Margaret would lead a procession, two by two, into the dining room. Even for ordinary family meals Muthesius observed that it was one of the immutable patterns of English life for the men to wear tails or dinner jackets and the women to be "décollettée" in evening dress. English country houses were planned so that this daily procession from the drawing room to the dining room would pass through the most imposing room, usually the hall, and Standen was no exception. Although

interconnecting doors between the adjacent rooms would have been more efficient, Webb planned the drawing room and dining room to necessitate a dignified route through the hall and along a short corridor, taking care to provide the servants with a separate passage to and from the kitchen. Servants carrying dishes arrived through a different doorway than the family and it was imperative that the two parties should never meet immediately before a meal.

At Standen, as was typical of the Arts and Crafts country house, the dining room was a focus for domestic ceremony and formal entertainment. The predominance of ritual and the palpable social hierarchies which were sharply defined around the table dictated a sober tone in its decoration and a meticulous attention to detail in the planning and furnishing of the room. The sideboard was designed and positioned for the convenience of the master of the house as well as servants delivering and removing dishes. Because the family's places at the table were absolutely fixed the room was positioned in the southeast corner as was convention. In this way Webb's plan avoided the horizontal rays of the setting sun through west-facing windows which, it was decreed, would have dazzled the diners: "The only sunlight that is welcome in the dining-room is that of the morning sun at breakfast." [26]

The English were obsessed with cooking smells and the corridor between kitchen and dining room at Standen was deliberately long, with bends built to avoid even a whiff from the kitchen permeating the family rooms. Food was kept warm on a slate shelf above a radiator between the kitchen corridor and the dining room; and high domed covers protected the dishes so that when they arrived in the dining room they were presented in puddles of condensation. However, the distance between the family rooms and those for the servants was an inflexible convention that even the most reforming architects were obliged to respect.

On the other side of the green baize door at Standen, a separate, intractable hierarchy determined the organization of the servants' wing. One of Webb's clients commented, when her house burned down, that it was a good thing their architect was a socialist because they were as comfortable living in the servants' quarters for a while as they had been in their own. The practical considerations of attracting and keeping good servants as well as political sympathies meant the majority of Arts and Crafts architects recognized that a generously equipped service wing was vital to the smooth running of a house.

The way that the Arts and Crafts house worked from the inside—the relationships between the different rooms, and their shapes, sizes, and orientations—determined the way that it looked from the outside. Webb did not show his clients any elevations for their houses until the plans were agreed upon. Unlike his contemporary, Richard Norman Shaw, who would begin by seducing the client with a magnificent perspective drawing, taking a worm's eye view to accentuate its dramatic features, Webb adhered to the Arts and Crafts conviction that the appearance of a building should express the different functions of the rooms within. Every detail of Standen can be rationalized by a quality of purpose or a sense of place. According to *Country Life* the mortar for the building was "mixed with brains."[27] Each elevation was composed and detailed to indicate the position of a staircase, for example, or to identify a clear relationship between conservatory and drawing room. *Country Life* explained to its readers that a conservatory "generally has an air altogether foreign, and gives the feeling that it is a disagreeable after-thought," but at Standen the massive brick arches and the low pitch roof, partly masked by a "bold lead gutter" are an integral part of the garden elevation. They were commended as "a masterly handling of a difficult problem."[28]

Webb's commitment to the preservation of ancient buildings and his determination to integrate the country house within the landscape caused him to invert the centuries-old architectural device used to create an imposing setting for a mansion. Laying a horizontal foil, a spacious turning circle in front of the entrance, was traditional, but there were no such concessions to magnificence at Standen. Instead Webb worked through a series of design revisions to incorporate a fifteenth-century farmhouse and one of its timber barns into a composition of buildings which frame the approach to the house.

The new service wing adopted the architectural language of modest agricultural dwellings and outbuildings and it was deliberately cranked to complement and consolidate the existing arrangement of old buildings and to articulate a roughly circular "House Green." Webb was poking fun, in a subtle, scholarly manner, at the ostentatious

ABOVE: Webb mixed materials and architectural references to local and historical styles in the elevations for Standen to create an impression of gracious propriety in the entrance front (left), with a rational and yet romantic informality in the garden elevation (right).

turning circle, but there was a more serious side to his allusion: that of a rural community gathered around a village green. Standen derives its name from one of three old farms which had occupied the site historically. At the center of an estate of three hundred acres with a substantial working farm, it maintained a traditional role as the nucleus of a working community. The indigenous building traditions and materials that gave the old farm buildings their distinctive architectural identity were threaded into the new design. This served as a gesture of continuity which related to the enduring responsibilities as well as the aesthetics of the Beales' new residence.

The materials for the house were quarried from the estate. The "soft and creamy Sussex stone streaked with rusty stains," which first appears as natural outcrops in sheer rock faces enclosing the approach road to the house, reappears in dressed form in its elevations.[29] It enhances the details of a covered arch that Webb designed to physically connect the old farmhouse with the new service wing at the opening to the entrance courtyard. Webb was a master in the craft of building and the time-honored tradition of using local materials was consolidated by the precision with which he instructed the builder. "The work for facing is to be done by axe, pick or broad chisel or all three according to circumstances. And the finished quality of the facing is to be of the kind shown in some old walling at the back of 'The Ship Inn,' East Grinstead."[30]

The Arts and Crafts ideal that a house should not be imposed upon the landscape but should appear to belong to it was exemplified at Standen. Webb insisted that the site the Beales had already leveled for the foundations of their new house prior to his appointment should be moved closer into the steep incline of the hillside. In this way, the contours of the building would harmonize with the natural topography of its surroundings. The north side of the entrance courtyard is closed by an almost sheer rocky bank, held in place by a stone retaining wall, creating a dramatic contrast between the dark formality of this enclosed space and the light open qualities of the House Green.

There was a general understanding among Arts and Crafts designers that the different faces of a building were a portrayal of their clients. Standen makes few concessions to prettiness but Halsey Ricardo suggested that the house was deliberately complex: "There should be romance, imagination and suggestion—something to attract one, some parts yet to be explored."[31] The entrance to Standen was described as "large, smiling and debonair, giving greeting to the incomer" and its northerly aspect, providing a constant light in the hall, the billiard room, and Mr. Beale's study, was considered ideal.[32] The garden elevation, facing south, articulates the private informality of the family's living spaces. It is poised to take advantage of spectacular views across the estate but is also, for this reason, the part of the building that relates most directly to the land and its history.

A row of five timber-clad gables breaks the roof line above passages of tile hanging between the first floor windows, making veiled references to the more elaborate tile hanging of the farmhouse and the timber barn. Webb used a gray Portland stone for the windowsills, while the window surrounds and arches to the conservatory are framed with hard red Keymer bricks. In less exposed places the local stone was mixed with red and gray stock bricks.[33] *Country Life* observed that, by mixing materials and by massing the projecting bays and steeply pitched roofs of the south and east elevations around a tower, Webb's composition negotiated a sympathetic relationship with its environment. "The house seems to have been built up bit by bit, almost unconsciously. Here is a bay built of the stone, quarried on the site, of a sober grey streaked with gold; there is a wall of the purplish Horsham brick; the tower is rough-cast, while part of the walls are hung with tiles and the gables filled with oak-boarding weathered to a silver grey. . .the final effect is to distract attention from any one feature and to leave on the consciousness a sense of large satisfaction for which one cannot quite account."[34]

The philosophy of Arts and Crafts, including a reverence for nature and its materials and the fusion of tradition and innovation, are exemplified by the planning and construction of Standen. The same ideals generated very different design solutions elsewhere in Britain and in America, however, and parallels can be drawn between houses which do not look alike. Between the town house and the country retreat entire suburbs were shaped by the Arts and Crafts Movement. The reforming spirit that rationalized the organization of the Victorian house also encompassed planning initiatives to check the unregulated sprawl of urban tenements and terraces. The term "town planning" was not coined until about 1906, by which time it was politically sensitive. Planning initiatives were well advanced, however, before town planning acts were tabled to abolish the slum and secure "the home healthy, the house beautiful, the town pleasant, the city dignified and the suburb salubrious."[35] The social and economic success of paternalistic "company towns" such as Bournville near Birmingham, England, built for employees of the Cadbury family in 1878, and the industrial town of Pullman, south of Chicago where workers at the Pullman factory were provided with parks, playgrounds, sports facilities, a library, and a theater as well as modest dwellings, encouraged garden city and garden suburb movements around the turn of the century to masterplan new communities.

Private developments as well as local government schemes created imaginative infrastructures within which individual houses could be commissioned or built speculatively. Entire areas, such as Highland Place in Berkeley and the area around Arroyo Terrace in Pasadena, California, revolved around the creative involvement of influential architects, and their distinctive designs attracted artistic clients. The way that houses were arranged on their plots and the consistent use of local or easily obtainable building materials extended the language of the Arts and Crafts house into the street. The architect Bernard Maybeck and his wife Annie insisted that the new roads to their hillside community in Berkeley should wind around existing trees, accentuating the rustic cabinlike qualities of Maybeck's redwood houses. The refined originality of Charles and Henry Greene's houses, which were elevated above the street and set back on their plots in Pasadena, proved so attractive that the Greenes had to design a gateway to the area in 1917 to keep interested tourists out. While there was status attached to the Greenes' extravagant commissions for wealthy clients, Maybeck's houses were simple and affordable. The Arts and Crafts house was not limited to exclusive designer suburbs. Roughcast rendered houses with steeply pitched roofs, leaded lights, and finely crafted details were discreetly inserted between Victorian villas. Craftsman bungalows and Prairie-style houses constructed to mail-order drawings coexisted with other fashionable styles of the period and within a mile or so of unique houses designed by famous architects to which their popular derivations paid homage.

The Arts and Crafts home signaled particular values and codes of behavior which cut across the boundaries of taste and class. In towns and suburbs, where buildings were clearly visible from the street, unconventional forms and materials amounted to a public statement about the characters and artistic inclinations of the inhabitants, which neighbors and passersby would have noted with curiosity or disapproval. Henry James, writing in 1878, described the decorative restraint of a fictional wooden house outside Boston with an insight into the language of architecture and a subtlety that was characteristic of the period. He likened its peaceful quietude and freshness to Quakerism

but it was identified, too, with a discreet form of professional success: "It's very clean! No splendors, no gilding, no troops of servants; rather straight-backed chairs . . .I should say there was wealth without symptoms. A plain, homely way of life; nothing for show, and very little for—what shall I call it?—for the senses; but a great aisance, and a lot of money, out of sight, that comes forward very quietly for subscriptions to institutions, for repairing tenements, for paying doctor's bills."[36]

Arts and Crafts houses were not always entirely in sympathy with their surroundings and the messages encoded in their elevations could be confrontational. The Glessner House was designed by H. H. Richardson for one of the most affluent suburbs in Chicago. The neighboring houses on Prairie Avenue housed some of the richest and most powerful men in the city including George Pullman and Marshall Field. In several respects the Glessners and their house can be compared with the Beales', at Standen. Where the design of Standen rejected the ostentation of earlier Victorian country houses, celebrating the rustic heritage of the site and its early buildings, the Glessner

LEFT AND ABOVE: Glessner House, H. H. Richardson, 1885–7, ground and first floor plans.

House encapsulates a different but equally coherent visual message. The open relationship between Standen and the landscape was emphatically closed at the Glessner House. It was nicknamed the "granite hut" by neighboring residents, but it was not the use of materials that caused offense. In one of his most forceful and innovative designs, Richardson redirected the architectural language of affluence to create the effect of a stronghold, fortified against the attentions of the street by the entrance front to the house. The rusticated stone façade pierced by small windows and an imposing arched entrance made learned references to the palazzos of the Italian Renaissance, buildings which were designed for the great merchants of Florence. The Glessner House, like the palazzos, fronted right onto the sidewalk with windows which were too high or too low to satisfy the curiosity of passersby.

The massive grids, chiseled out of granite to screen the ground floor windows, cocked a snook at the conventional good manners of the neighboring houses, which were set back from the street and turned politely to face it. The architectural

language of the Italian palazzo with its resonances of wealth, stability, and security was commonplace as a model for city banks and insurance companies in the late nineteenth century, where its associations were used to positive effect. By using the same associations in a domestic dwelling, however, Richardson made a provocative and sophisticated comment about contemporary power bases founded on trade.

H. H. Richardson (1838–1886) was one of the earliest American architects to consciously strive toward a monumental form of architecture which would express the American spirit. Like most of his contemporaries, he was trained at the Beaux Arts and his early buildings followed the prevailing fashions for English Victorian Gothic and French Second Empire styles. In his mature work, however, Richardson remodeled the components of Romanesque architecture to arrive at a powerful and robust style; the bold massing of his work was likened to his immense girth and stature as a man. When a German enthusiast exclaimed, "*Mein Gott*, how he looks like his own buildings," Richardson was amused, answering that "it was a great thing to be monumental."[37]

His clients in Chicago, John and Frances Glessner, like the Beales, combined commercial success with an active interest in the arts. John Glessner was forty-two and a partner in the firm of Warder, Bushnell and Glessner, manufacturers of farming machinery, when he commissioned the house. Frances, the mother of their two children, was a trained teacher and an accomplished pianist. She was actively involved in the Decorative Arts Society and John Glessner served on the board of directors of the Art Institute of Chicago and later became a patron of the Chicago Symphony Orchestra. The Glessner House was a winter home and, because of its proximity to the city, a setting for lavish entertainment.[38] Receptions were given for more than four hundred people at a time and on special occasions the entire Chicago Symphony Orchestra entertained the Glessners at home. The rooms were neither grand nor particularly large, though, because Richardson adapted planning conventions to create a house that was responsive to the Glessner's public responsibilities as influential hosts while retaining the domestic intimacy of a home for a small family.

Like Philip Webb, Richardson planned his houses from the inside out, first ascertaining how the clients wanted to live in the house and then drawing up a floor plan before the elevations were even considered. The principal rooms in the Glessner House face south and west to take advantage of the winter sunshine and the house is inward looking, gathered around a courtyard garden in a U-shaped plan that turns its back on its urban setting. Instead of raising the front door above street level by an external flight of steps Richardson set the massive front door on a single stone plinth, anchoring the building to the ground. A wide flight of steps immediately inside an internal porch defines a ceremonial ascent to the living hall, raised above a semibasement and a majestic staircase leading directly off the hall extends the space upward to a galleried landing on the first floor. This pinwheeling momentum upward through the house—with the hall as a magnetic focus to be anticipated from below and overheard and overlooked from the landing above—is balanced by a lateral pull from the hall into the principal rooms on the raised ground floor. Generous openings between the hall, the parlor, and the dining room enabled these three adjoining rooms to overflow into one another as a fluid sequence of spaces "without any feeling of crush, confusion or heat" when hundreds of guests attended musical recitals and dramatic readings at the house.[39] Individually, however, the rooms were scaled and decorated with warm colors and oak paneling for more intimate family occasions.

In keeping with town-house conventions the library is located at the front of the house overlooking the street, immediately to the right of the main entrance. There is no differentiation in Richardson's front elevation (as there is at Standen) between this semi-public room used for business and private study, and the more intimate space of the master bedroom which matches it symmetrically on the opposite side of the front door. While the Classical face of the building masks the organization of its interior from the street, however, the way that the rooms were used, as well as their location within the house, abandoned normal codes of practice. The traditional male preserve of the library was shared equally between John and Frances Glessner, furnished with a massive desk at which they sat facing one another to work. Most society hostesses entertained in the drawing room but every Monday morning for more than thirty years the ladies of Prairie Avenue and wives of the faculty of the University of Chicago congregated in the library for Mrs. Glessner's reading class.[40]

The master bedroom was at the center of a vertical stack of rooms in its own south wing, which Richardson arranged as a private apartment within the house where family relationships and domestic routines were set apart from the distractions and upheaval of social events. The master bedroom overlooking the street was sandwiched between the children's schoolroom in the semibasement and their two bedrooms on the floor above. All three floors were linked by their own spiral staircase. Although the bedroom corridors opened onto the hall on the upper ground floor, Richardson curved the southwest wall of the hall so that visitors would be drawn toward the fireplace and the living room, away from the family's private quarters.

The degree to which an architect discerns the personal requirements of a client intuitively, and the extent to which these are specified during the meetings and discussions that lead to a commission, is seldom documented. A close friendship developed between the Glessner and Richardson families between their first meeting in

May 1885 and the architect's death less than a year later; some aspects of the design of the Glessner House are described or alluded to in the unpublished journals and accounts of John and Frances Glessner. New houses designed for their friends played a part in shaping the brief and the Glessner House was unashamedly shown off when it was first completed. "Talking house" was commonplace between the Glessners and their friends, and a few weeks before the first meeting with Richardson, Frances Glessner's journal describes a visit by one of his other clients: "Mrs MacVeagh came over to show us the plans of her new house. . .she explained all to us and then very kindly left them with us over Sunday."[41]

John Glessner later recalled that they selected Richardson for his reputation as "America's foremost architect at that time."[42] Instead of a written brief he took Richardson to his present home: "I could tell him in half an hour what it would take a day to do elsewhere," but when Richardson asked how Glessner wanted the rooms arranged he protested. "Oh, no, Mr Richardson, that would be me planning the house. I want you to plan it. That's your job. If we don't like it we'll change it."[43] Richardson was too incapacitated by ill health and obesity to get out of the carriage when Glessner drove him to look at the site for the new house, "but looked at the place attentively and in silence some minutes."[44] Glessner's recollection of the planning of the house over dinner the following evening describes a reverential attitude toward the architect as creative genius, relieved by an affection for his weaknesses as a man which has all the makings of a classic design legend. "While the last course of our dinner was being removed before dessert, he called for pencil and paper. . .he rapidly drew the first floor plan, almost exactly as it was finally decided on. The dessert was strawberry shortcake, for which our cook was famous. He asked for a second piece, with the added remark— 'Mrs Glessner, that's the best pie I ever put in my mouth.'"[45]

The organization of Richardson's houses was far from standardized and the imaginative planning of the Glessner House was perfectly attuned to the clients' slightly unconventional requirements. The grouping of rooms into vertical and horizontal alignments and the spatial dynamics through three dimensions around the hall reconciled the public and private functions of the house, but Richardson's innovations were couched in traditional references. The Glessner House combines elements of the conventional town house with the more relaxed, virtuoso planning of a country retreat. The hall and library at the front of the house provided a formal introduction to the interior while the direct relationship between the living room and the dining room was typical of American country houses. American clients took a healthier attitude toward cooking smells than their English contemporaries; the kitchen at the Glessner House is separated from the dining room only by the butler's pantry, where food was set out ready for serving. The gloomy formality of English dining was also contradicted by an immense bay window, admitting fresh air and winter sunshine throughout the day. Richardson ran a corridor from the kitchen to the hall, serving all the principal rooms between, but it was intended for the servants' use rather than for formal processions into dinner.

Although they were very different architecturally, there are parallels between the Glessner House and Standen that illuminate wider connections between the English and American Arts and Crafts movements. Both houses were furnished with Morris & Co. patterns and furniture. The decoration of Standen was an obvious expression of the relationship between Morris and Webb: "Morris was the man Webb wanted to complete the houses he built" and, according to May Morris, Webb's houses were among those that Morris cared most about "and understood how to make into beautiful homes."[46] Richardson, too, had met Morris during a visit to England in 1882 when he sought out Morris & Co.'s new factory at Merton Abbey. He wrote, "Mr. William Morris happened to be in, and he went personally with us over the works and gave extremely interesting accounts of the progress he had made in the manufacture of his glass, carpets, stuffs, etc."[47] The following Sunday Richardson was invited to Kelmscott House, "and the five-o'clock tea there. . .with the various 'aesthetes' was an experience long to be remembered."[48] He was introduced to the ceramicist William De Morgan and he visited Edward Burne-Jones at his home.

Richardson died before the Glessner House was completed. The Glessners, who had visited his home and office in Boston, consciously emulated their architect's taste by using ceramics by De Morgan and textiles by Morris which they had seen there. A portière in his library designed by Morris was replicated exactly at the Glessner House, and although the Glessners acquired Morris papers and fabrics through department stores and other American suppliers, like the Beales they prided themselves on a direct relationship with William Morris. John Glessner later wrote that the library portière which Frances Glessner embroidered "had the pattern draw on the silk by Mr Morris's own hand," and that the Hammersmith rugs were woven especially for the house.[49] Margaret Beale also embroidered Morris patterns for Standen, however, in both houses Morris & Co. furnishings were mixed with furniture designed by other architects so that they reflected the clients' tastes rather than an interior dictated by the architect.

The Glessners regarded the building of their house as a material reflection of the memories and events that distinguished their lives as well as a monument to Richardson's genius. They believed that their home was the one which, of all his commissions, Richardson would have most liked to live in himself. They were equally convinced that the design had been inspired by a small photograph of an old stone building in Abingdon, near Oxford, England, which Richardson had picked up from the mantel in their library. "Do you like that?" he had asked. "Well give it to me: I'll make that the keynote of your house."[50] Even the blot of ink which marked the photograph when it was returned to them after Richardson's death is mentioned in Glessner's "Story of a House" as evidence of the creative relationship between the architect and his client.

The photograph describes some of the differences as well as the affiliations between English and American Arts and Crafts. Where Webb's individual style became absorbed in the scholarly adaptation of local and historical references, in Richardson's work architectural allusions were transformed to meet what he perceived to be the demands of the age and his own distinctive originality. The stone gables and the long, undifferentiated contour of a Cotswold terrace provided him with a foil for the Classical

RIGHT: Richardson drew his
inspiration for the Glessner House
from a photograph of buildings in the
Cotswolds, England.

regularity and near-symmetry of the Prairie Avenue elevation. They were enlarged and
adapted into a Richardsonian statement in the side elevation of the Glessner House,
executed in the same massive blocks of rough-cut granite as the entrance front. The side
elevation was designed to express the transition from family rooms to service
accommodation, with the library at one end and a row of narrow vertical windows
denoting the service corridor, which had its own dramatic trade entrance. However, the
identification of a modern American style of architecture was more important in the
Glessner House elevations than an accurate representation of the internal plan or a
testimonial to English building traditions.

Toward the end of his life John Glessner described the concept of the home as a
refuge from the restless uncertainties of the age, reiterating the popular ideal of the rural
manor as a symbol of continuity, which *The House* magazine had presented to its
readers in 1897. "I think the desire is in us all to receive the family home from the past
generation and hand it on to the next with possibly some good mark of our own upon
it. Rarely can this be accomplished in this land of rapid changes. Families have not held
and cannot hold even to the same localities for their homes generation after generation
but we can at least preserve some memory of the old."[51] The image of a traditional stone
dwelling in the Cotswolds which Glessner presented to Richardson belongs to the same
architectural vocabulary as Kelmscott Manor. It manifested the same cultural references
to the home as an immutable emblem of permanence, security, and stability which were
fundamental to the work of Morris and Webb. In the design of the Glessner House,
however, Richardson magnified the quintessential elements of "the home," coupling the
authority and stability of Classical architecture with the unassuming traditions of an
English manor house to produce an iconic urban statement.

MAKING AN ENTRANCE

THE FIRST CLUES TO the character of an Arts and Crafts house were consciously laid out in the path to the front door. In the English country retreat a lodge close to the road often paraphrased the architectural style of the main building and the house itself was concealed behind high walls or hedges. Good connections, according to Muthesius, were necessary "to break the spell of its privacy" and enter "the fairy-tale world" which was fabricated around the house and its gardens.[1] American country houses of a comparable value were more open in their relationships with the world outside. They distanced themselves from the curiosity of passersby by their positions, set back and often elevated on their plots, but they were designed to assert an aesthetic superiority over the neighborhood, while their English counterparts were discreetly hidden away.

In the town and suburban house, the route to the front door was shorter and the ways in which a designer and his clients could compose an evocative setting for the house were more limited. The psychology of arrival, nevertheless, was carefully considered, even in the most modest suburban houses. C.F.A. Voysey advised his fellow architects: "You will express decision and determination by forming a straight path or drive from the road to the house, making it wide to suggest hospitality and welcome, and avoiding

LEFT AND RIGHT: Thackeray Turner designed Westbrook in Surrey for his own family in 1899–1900. He was profoundly influenced by Webb and his insistence upon good traditional materials and expert craftsmanship, rooted in his work as secretary to the Society for the Preservation of Ancient Buildings, are exemplified in the treatment of the living hall (left) and the construction of the staircase (right) from solid pieces of timber.

any wobbling indecision, which only suggests weakness."[2] Voysey's doors were wide in proportion to height, recalling Tudor traditions, "not stand offishly dignified, like a coffin lid, high and narrow for the entrance of one body only."[3] An emphasis on craftsmanship, accentuating the grain of massive planks of oak and the structure of the door, hung on wrought-iron strap hinges, set the tone for the use of fine materials and the decorative integrity of the interiors.

The Arts and Crafts hall was regarded as the key to the planning and decoration of the entire house. As an interchange between the different rooms it was central to the organization of the interior but it was also a threshold between the public face of the building and its private interiors. The experience of entering the house was consciously designed as the culmination of all the impressions gathered between the first glimpse of the building and the opening of the front door. Principles of architectural integrity and unity were put to the test by the consistent use of materials and motifs and the way in which the historic references and cultural allusions that shaped the form and character

of the exterior were developed or abandoned inside. The hall provided an interlude in which to adjust to the process of entry but it also served as a waiting room where messengers were received and calling cards were deposited. Not everybody who was admitted into the hall would be invited into the drawing room. To make matters more complicated, the formalities of the hall as an introduction to the house were juxtaposed against its most intimate comings and goings. Early morning visitors were in danger of encountering the housemaid carrying chamber pots and bathwater down from the bedrooms in progressive houses where secondary servants' staircases were omitted.

In Victorian houses the hall was often treated as a vacuous space, extravagantly designed to create an impression of grandeur or else neglected, "little better than a conduit pipe or flue, through which guests might be shot into the reception rooms as speedily as possible."[4] Its utilitarian functions remained unchanged throughout the Arts and Crafts period and very little could be done to standardize the variety of different shapes and sizes dictated by different houses—ranging from baronial proportions to the long narrow passage with a staircase "like a toboggan slide" facing the front door. The hall was reinvented, nevertheless, by the Arts and Crafts Movement. It became a focus for radical innovations, announcing the reforming principles of its clients and designers. Although the practical characteristics of the Victorian hall, the use of dark colors, hard-wearing surfaces, and the necessary furniture and ornamental potted plants could not be dispensed with entirely, they were redefined within more usable, welcoming spaces, designed to create an impression of candor and hospitality.

Each successive stage in the process of arrival was analyzed and accentuated, so that the path to the front door, the shelter of a porch, the door itself, and then the opening of the interior space were conceived as cumulative experiences. Open porches, partly framed by the walls of the house and screened by climbing plants, expressed an interlocking relationship between the exterior and interior of the Arts and Crafts house and its relationship with nature. In hot climates where the roof of the house extended forward to shelter a veranda where its occupants could sit out in the evenings, watching the life of the street, the division between the public and private spaces of the home and the formalities of entry were erased. Craftsman houses were designed with deep front porches to give a sense of protection and enclosure between the street and the front door. Their timbers were exposed to accentuate the sturdiness of their structure and to soften the solid planes of the building, but they also broke conventions and generated new, informal patterns in lifestyle. They distilled the most desirable elements of a relaxed, colonial affluence into a form that every homeowner could afford.

OPPOSITE LEFT: Terraced houses in Ruskin Avenue, Kew, were designed to introduce color and variety to the streetscape.

OPPOSITE RIGHT: Individually designed houses by Cavendish Pearson brought a distinctive, artistic character to the Brentham Estate in Ealing.

In less favorable climates where "the charm of living out of doors" was negligible for much of the year, a shallow outer porch protected the front door from wind and rain.[5] In both the bungalow developments of California and the speculative houses of English suburban streets, however, the porch was calculated to create an effect of welcome and to highlight the artistic refinement of the area. Stained-glass doors with ornamental tile surrounds and the combined effects of bay windows and porch recesses, framed by painted timber architraves and lintels, introduced color and variety to the streetscape. The importance of the porch to the exterior of the house was evenly matched by its usefulness in shielding the hall from drafts and providing an external lobby for outdoor clothes and equipment. This dual role, enabling even the smallest hall to be treated as a living space, was considered so indispensable to the comfort and convenience of the home that in houses where no adequate outer porch could be provided, an inner porch was often installed as a dust and dirt lobby.

Innovations which were pioneered in architect-designed houses were simplified and adapted to more ordinary needs. *The House* offered its readers a detailed specification for an inner porch furnished as a miniature room, recommending that even the rented house would benefit from a timber screen, constructed across the hall passage a few feet from the front door with a secondary door "fitted with some prettily leaded, glistening white, or creamy opaque glass."[6] A large mat with a boot cleaner was recommended to give the first note of welcome and plain hooks fastened beneath a strong oak shelf were suggested "for the reception of such waterproofs and coats as are barred from the inner hall."[7] Readers were warned against tasteless excesses around the front door: "Beware of the more hideous forms of so-called painted or stained glass, rich in unnatural kingfishers and conventional robins" and, where space permitted, an oak bench was advocated "for persons whom it is not desirable to admit beyond this first fortification."[8] These inner porches made discreet references to the antechambers of medieval manors, an image perpetuated by the more elaborate porch and cloakroom facilities of country houses which catered to the needs of visitors arriving for longer visits after arduous journeys. By relegating hats, coats, and the odd messenger to the porch, even a narrow passage came close to the status of a "living hall" from which pegs and racks were absolutely banished.

The idea of the front door as a statement of individuality was perfected by Arts and Crafts designers. Its pictorial qualities as a flat, rectangular plane in front of which waiting visitors would stand, and its emblematic significance as a boundary to be opened or closed were explored in subtle compositions which called familiar components and materials into service as *objets d'art*. The proportions of the door and the use of oak and other hardwoods, which had been selected for their natural beauty and hand finished to reveal the processes of craftsmanship, consciously evoked the values of Arts and Crafts. Carved rails, art glass panels, and fine metalwork brought together in distinctive but aesthetically balanced arrangements, exemplified the principle of unity between the arts. The details of a front door occasionally disclosed an aspect of its owner's or its maker's personality. Voysey's heart-shaped letter plates symbolized a profound spiritual love which he believed to be the source of creativity. When H. G. Wells, who was a philanderer as well as an atheist, commissioned a Voysey house and told his architect that he objected to wearing his heart on his front door, the letter plate was inverted and given a tail and the house was named Spade House. Wells was fortunate not to have been given horns and caricatured elsewhere in the joinery of the house, as some of Voysey's other clients had been.[9]

RIGHT: Front door to The Homestead in Essex, designed by Voysey in 1905–6.

ABOVE: Stained glass was used in jewel-like abstract patterns and larger, figurative designs in Arts and Crafts front doors. This example from a 1920s town house describes the enduring ideal of a whitewashed cottage in the country as a symbol for Home.

Symbols were used extensively in Arts and Crafts designs to express shared values and to convey meanings and messages among a cognoscenti that might offend or perplex the unenlightened. C. R. Ashbee's door knockers, fashioned for the house which he designed for himself and his mother in Cheyne Walk in London, were daringly idiosyncratic in a period when, as Wilde found to his cost, homosexuality remained a criminal offense. They were modeled in the form of two naked boys "with every detail shown to perfection." [10] An artistic front door was not necessarily attached to an architect-designed house, though. The application of fine craftsmanship and creative originality to ordinary domestic objects which the Arts and Crafts Movement promoted made art metalwork available to ordinary householders. Voysey's heart-shaped letter plate could be purchased for one pound and five shillings, together with bell pushes, barrel bolts, locks, latches, and hinges from a catalog of domestic metalwork made to his designs by Thomas Elsley Limited in London. Stickley's Craftsman Workshops in America manufactured and marketed metal furnishings and readers of *The Craftsman* were encouraged to craft their own door hardware: "Metal work is one of the most interesting of the crafts to the home worker who possesses skill and taste and, above all, a genuine interest in making for himself the things that are needed either for use or ornament at home."[11]

The highly polished precision of conventional door hardware was deliberately challenged by the irregular forms of base-metal hinges and handles. A unanimous directive from Arts and Crafts designers that the deep mellow browns and the greenish tints of copper and brass left free from lacquer should be allowed to harmonize with unpolished oak—"age and exposure being the only agents required to produce beauty and variety of tone"—contradicted the most obvious demonstrations of the efficiently run household literally reflected in the gleaming details of the front door.[12] It corresponded, however, with an appeal for reform in household management. The necessity of standing half in and half out of the house, holding the door open to polish its brass fittings before kneeling to scrub the front step "at least three hundred days in the year" was condemned by progressive women writers as an insufferable archaism ruinous to women's health. "On cold winter mornings the process is unpleasant for everybody, and at all times labour is wasted."[13]

Although painted doors which were grained to look like wood or marble were rejected by the Arts and Crafts Movement as "distasteful to all truth-loving and really Artistic intellects," plain painted colors provided an economic alternative to hardwood doors.[14] Even in rented houses the artistic householder was encouraged to discard the handle, bell-pull, and knocker from the front door ("carefully storing them in the lumber room until the end of the tenancy") before repainting the front door in a color which would complement both the new art metalwork and the surrounding walls.[15] *The House* magazine recommended a dull peacock blue as a contrast to yellowish stock bricks and Venetian red or "deep olive-green paint, relieved with bronze or copper or brass fittings" for red brick houses.[16] Lanterns, often designed by the same art metalwork suppliers, were hung within the porch recess or suspended from brackets to one side to complete the impression of welcome and stylish distinction, but it was not until the door was opened and the interior space revealed that the assembly of images and impressions laid along the path to the front door could be appreciated as elements in a comprehensive vision.

At the Gamble House in Pasadena, California, designed by Greene and Greene between 1907 and 1909, the creative originality and craftsmanship that distinguish the entire building are clearly stated in the view of the house from the street. Deliberately set on a sculpted lawn modeled to create a curvaceous platform for the building, the open structure of sleeping porches balanced by the more formal, closed massing of a guest wing indicate an interest in Japanese design which informed an ideological as well as a stylistic approach to the house. The landscaping conceals the line of the driveway and creepers cover the risers to a wide flight of steps leading to the front door so that from the front, the house has an immaculate detachment like an island surrounded by green. For visitors, however, this initial impression of restrained authority is immediately supplanted by a sequence of dramatic perspectives and surface textures, brought into sharp relief by the crescent-shaped driveway, which ensures that the house is approached from an increasingly oblique angle. A rhythm of projecting planes, deep overhanging eaves, and exposed beams and rafter tails is sharply defined in light and shade. The natural colors and textures of the timber structure and shingle cladding contrast against the red bricks of the drive, laid in a chevron formation that gives way to narrower, biscuit-brown bricks in the steps to the house.

A wide terrace, wrapping around three sides of the house and partially covered by its sleeping porches, acts as a foil to the monumental art glass front door, but it also gave access to Mr. Gamble's den and to the drawing room, so that the formalities of arrival and departure through the hall could be bypassed by the family and their most intimate friends. Pasadena was a popular resort for midwesterners; the Gamble House was a winter retreat for David and Mary Gamble and their two sons. It was designed to maximize the advantages of the California climate and to accommodate a relaxed lifestyle but the covered terrace at the front of the Gamble House was not designed as a sitting-space where the family could laze outside in the evenings. The orientation of the house was designed to fill each space with sunshine during the hours that family routines and standard conventions dictated that the particular room or terrace would be in use, and the front of the house, facing east, lights up in the early morning.

The front terrace served as an extension to Mr. Gamble's study space and its distance from the front door was deliberate. The terrace and sleeping porches on the garden side of the house overlooking the Arroyo Seco were used by the family in the evenings. Although the front of the house gives the impression of openness and informality, the Gambles' social status—their immense family fortune emanated from the Proctor and Gamble soap manufacturing business—was upheld by the majestic gravity of the front door.

Framed in a gold-colored teakwood, which contrasts with the soft greenish brown timber of the shingles, the image of an ancient California oak, designed by Charles Greene and executed in layers of iridescent art glass by Emil Lange, is spread across a composition of three doors and the lights above them. A wide, recessed central front door is flanked by a pair of screen doors flush with the frame. The doors provide a dramatic focus that consolidates the emphatic horizontals of the front elevation and binds its asymmetrical arrangement together. An unobtrusive brass latch, key escutcheon, and bell push contribute to the impression of fine craftsmanship and rich surface textures; a lantern suspended from one of the beam ends above the door makes an obvious reference to the delicate linearity and cropped compositions of Japanese design. The satisfactions of arrival are arrested, however, by the leading of the glass panels which articulates the doublesided nature of the door. The tree is designed to be viewed from the interior and it is not until the door is opened and the threshold is crossed that the allusions to Japanese design and the sensuous presentation of a succession of colors and textures, natural materials, and artistically manufactured effects are resolved into a definitive statement.

The screen doors provided ventilation, but for Charles Greene a composition of three doors may have represented a mystical trinity which, with the dual nature of the

ABOVE: Greene and Greene designed the approach to the Gamble House along a crescent-shaped red brick path so that the building would be experienced as a succession of finely crafted materials and textures, culminating in the art glass front door.

door and the overall unity of the design, suggest an early reference to his later interest in the ancient wisdom of theosophy.[17] This abstract symbolism supplements a more accessible, pictorial reading of the front door as an image of constancy and change within nature. Silhouetted against the transitory brilliance of a sunrise, the tree, rooted in the earth, suggests a structure of enduring stability. This allusion is reiterated by the way that sunlight filters through the door each morning to illuminate the hall, marking the passage of time by the gradual rotation of golden reflections through the space.

The idea that the complete house should be conceived and crafted as a work of art is clearly articulated in the Gamble House hall. The creative originality of Greene and

ABOVE: Looking east with the drawing room to the left, the Gamble House hall with morning sunlight streaming through the art glass front door.

Greene's design complied, nevertheless, with the conventions of the period and, although they were modified to meet the informal lifestyle and climate of a California holiday home, the standard finishes and furniture of an ordinary nineteenth-century hall are found in the Gamble House. The effect of warmth and hospitality that Muthesius described as essential to the Arts and Crafts hall was achieved through the use of light in the mornings without the unnecessary heat of an open fire. It is sustained throughout the day by the rich tones of the dark Burma teak paneling which covers the walls to frieze height. Paneling was the most traditional wall treatment for a hall, but the usual practice of lining all the walls with a uniform pattern was disregarded at the Gamble

House. The paneling on the south wall is so simplistic that it is reduced to the most rudimentary framing beneath a broad picture rail, which is shafted to display the joiner's skill and to suggest a superfluous expression of strength. In contrast, the joinery around the staircase on the north side of the hall is assembled to exhibit the most exacting standards of craftsmanship through an elaborate interpretation of the structure of the staircase, rising in three distinct flights through the space.

The Arts and Crafts hall was furnished to accommodate the rituals of arrival. The social convention of the "At Home," by which visitors (mainly women) paid short social calls to one another's homes in the afternoons, determined the arrangement of the room. There was a sturdy hall table where letters and calling cards were deposited when the householder was not at home and where visitors' outdoor clothes were carefully folded and laid. Social callers could see at a glance whether their friends and rivals were already ensconced in the drawing room by the arrangement on the hall table. (In larger houses a cloakroom was provided where guests arriving for longer periods could leave their outdoor clothes and wash.) Having announced their arrival in the form of a calling card, visitors would wait to be received into the drawing room or the library, and in colder climates comfortable chairs, upholstered in leather for waiting guests, were drawn around an open fire "in which the logs burn[ed] brightly, and thro[e]w a pretty glow over the walls and furniture." [18] One or two more utilitarian wooden chairs were placed close to the front door "for messengers and the like" and individual styles of furniture

BELOW; Gamble House, Greene and Greene, 1907–9, ground and first floor plans.

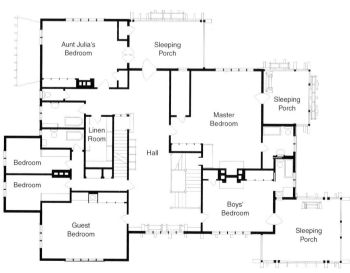

were weighted with moral as well as social implications.[19] One nineteenth-century writer described the hard and slippery hall seat as "a stool of repentance," installed as a protest "by the well-to-do-classes against undue luxury in those beneath them."[20]

The Gamble House hall is furnished with a hall table and a pair of chairs designed by the Greenes and upholstered in leather. A corner seat built into the L-shaped structure of the staircase provided seating for waiting visitors and messengers alike. This exquisitely crafted bench adapts the model of the hall settle which was popularized by the Arts and Crafts Movement, recalling the rustic forms of medieval furniture. A chest was incorporated into the seat, in keeping with historic prototypes, and a Victorian taste for strategically placed potted plants in the hall was neatly accommodated by an arm rest that doubled as a marble-topped plinth. The seat was not designed with comfort as a priority but it played a crucial role in defining a formal waiting area within the overall space of the hall. Visitors sat facing the front door with their backs turned to the finely crafted enclosure of the staircase and the family rooms beyond. The Greenes provided a coat closet opposite the bench, and the bathroom to a guest bedroom on the ground floor at the front of the house was economically planned so that it was also available to visitors arriving at the house.

Although the Gamble House hall was planned as a generous circulation space at the heart of the building, it was designed and furnished to separate the different regions of the house and, at the same time, to promote a sense of unity and correspondence between its different parts. The candor with which the full depth of the house is immediately revealed to visitors through the glazed doors leading into the garden, directly opposite the front door, is tempered by a subtle division of the long, broadly rectangular space into two parts. The waiting area is sandwiched between Mr. Gamble's study and the guest bedroom at the front of the house but beyond the projecting treads to the staircase a more informal space is defined between the living room and the garden. There are no doors between the wide opening to the living room and this more intimate, west end of the hall, and the piano was positioned just inside the living-room partition so that the two spaces could function together when large or disparate groups gathered in the house. The hall was wide to establish a neutral space between the family rooms on the north side of the house and the service wing to the south. The delicate balance between free-flowing spaces and private enclosures is exemplified in the arrangement of the dining room in the southwest corner of the plan, at the furthest extreme from the front door. Sliding doors between the hall and this more private family space meant that it could be opened or closed according to the occasion.

The Gamble House is a sophisticated and a mature example of an Arts and Crafts hall in which the disparate functions of the space are reconciled within a compelling artistic statement. By removing the physical boundaries between different rooms it accommodated more open and flexible patterns in behavior and the "artistic" styling of the space and its fittings legitimized the clients' progressive lifestyle and attitudes toward decorum. The Greenes' references to the architecture of Japan gave the house a fashionably exotic edge and carried an enduring vogue for blue-and-white china and for Japanese prints and garden structures into a new dimension.

RIGHT: The structure of the staircase is exalted through exquisite craftsmanship and stylized detailing to suggest a symbolic significance.

The hall suggested spiritual affiliations, however, as well as announcing the artistic orientation of the home as a complete environment. The elaborate expression of structure and the sculptural handling of joinery details around the stairs are weighted with implied meaning, and the Greenes included a pictorial symbol in the pendant light fittings at the east and west ends of the hall. Rose and crane motifs incised into their wooden frames make reference to the Gambles' family crest but the crane is also a symbol of longevity in Japanese design. A sculpted crane from the Gambles' collection was suspended from one of the staircase corbels.

The temples and teahouses that inspired the design of the Gamble House were spiritual and ceremonial spaces. American designers in particular looked to Japanese sources as alternatives to the overworked traditions of European architectural styles, and the complex associations between decoration and meaning which underpinned the Arts and Crafts Movement meant that houses which interpreted Asian forms were often invested with meditative and transcendental readings. As single-cell buildings, the temple and the teahouse exerted a particular fascination for American architects. They extended an existing repertoire of domestic models, loaded with cultural associations, which were called upon to redefine the Arts and Crafts hall. The medieval hall house, the hunting lodge, and the most basic rural cottages and cabins were idealized as dwellings which revolved around multipurpose halls. At the Gamble House and in earlier English country houses by Webb and Shaw where the ideal of the living hall was invented, the styling and structure of these historic spaces were recalled for their cultural as well as their architectural associations. In these relatively affluent houses, however, the hall was designed as an addition to the living room and dining room. It was a space for entertaining: for music and pageants and afternoon tea, even for dancing and billiards (although the Gambles, who were strict Presbyterians, disapproved of such things), a place where conventional codes of behavior could be bent or broken.

A romantic nostalgia for what was remembered as the simple life and for the courtly rituals of medieval legends, made popular by Pre-Raphaelite paintings and Arthurian tales, was translated into picturesque interiors at the social heart of the house which set the scene for flamboyant or artistically refined behavior. The living hall at Blackwell, designed by Baillie Scott in 1898 for a hillside site overlooking Lake Windermere in Cumbria, a county in northwest England, was furnished with a massive inglenook fireplace beneath a half-timbered minstrel's gallery. For Baillie Scott, however, these sentimental allusions to a bygone age were inseparable from a vision of the ancient hall as "the most primitive form of plan," which could be revived and reformed as the nucleus of the modern house.[21] "It was there the family cooked and ate their food. It was there they talked. And when night came it was on its rush-strewn floor that they slept."[22] The responsibility of the modern architect, he claimed, "with his essentially modern historical sense," was to reconsider the hall as a gathering place which could supplement or even replace other rooms in the house.

The hall at Blackwell was at the center of the plan, with the drawing room on one side and the dining room on the other, and it was separated from the front door by a wide corridor "so that it never becomes a passage-room."[23] Conceived as an extravagant gesture "aping the large house" in an otherwise modestly scaled six-bedroom home, it combined the grandeur of an Elizabethan hunting lodge (a model conveniently free from restrictive associations as far as codes of behavior were concerned) with a meticulously planned arrangement of open spaces and enclosures, designed to accommodate all the indoor activities of country life within a single room.[24] Muthesius praised Baillie Scott as a poet whose "ravishing ideas of spatial organization" insured that every part of the house "down to the smallest corner, is thought out as a place to be lived in." The "hall-living-room" at Blackwell was commended as a comfortable all-purpose room "in which each member of the family can follow his favourite pursuit and spend his time as he likes."[25]

The formalities of arrival were taken care of in a separate porch and cloakroom so that the transition from the corridor into a vast double-height space, dramatically decorated with exposed beams and timber studs, was designed to impress. An elegant bench was arranged immediately inside the door for waiting visitors (messengers would have been confined to the porch), and early photographs show the door itself covered by a portière—an embroidered or woven hanging designed to keep out drafts. In later photographs the chairs were replaced by bookcases and a piano, suggesting that activities confined to the drawing room and the library in more conventional houses were allowed to spill over into the hall.

Arts and Crafts designers were adept at creating rooms within rooms by altering floor and ceiling heights and by using electric light fittings to accentuate particular areas such

LEFT AND ABOVE: The "billiard-room recess" (left) and the staircase with its enclosed landing built alongside the main inglenook (above) were designed as intimate enclosures within the vast hall at Blackwell.

as reading alcoves and dining tables. In a pioneering piece of social as well as spatial integration, Baillie Scott designed a "billiard-room recess" for the hall at Blackwell. The ceiling height at the east end of the room, closest to the dining room, was lowered and the billiard table was lit by a specialized fitting, known at the turn of the century as an extrolier (a special six-lamp fitting over a billiard table). The carved paneling at one end of the table was boxed around a bench seat from which the game could be watched or ignored and at the other end a deep splay-sided bay opened into the garden. The initial focus of attention, however, drawing visitors into the hall, was the monumental chimneypiece, faced with an interlocking pattern of local slate and stone above an old-fashioned delft tile surround. Baillie Scott provided a bay window with its own built-in seat within the inglenook so that this much smaller room within a room could be used for reading and chatting by the warmth of the fire throughout the day.

Opinions were divided among designers and critics about the place of the staircase in the living hall. Muthesius observed that a conspicuous staircase within the hall was the mark of a public building rather than a dwelling. It invited curiosity about the bedrooms, which were regarded as absolutely private, and it promoted drafts—"and there are plenty of these already."[26] In houses large enough to warrant servants but too small to justify a secondary staircase, there were obvious organizational problems in opening the only staircase into one of the principal living spaces rather than housing it in a separate vestibule. Designers and their clients were seduced, however, by the advantages of absorbing the area taken up by the staircase into the usable living space of the hall, and in the holiday houses where living halls took hold, the issue of drafts was less problematic. The staircase and its screen of balustrades presented opportunities for theatrical effects in both the design of the room and the behavior of its occupants. Its position, tucked into one of the corners of the room or prominently arranged to direct attention upward, became a creative component in the spatial dynamics of the room. Baillie Scott believed that the main staircase should be either enclosed within the hall or "banished from it altogether."[27]

Blackwell was large enough to incorporate a secondary staircase; this narrow flight of stairs set alongside the inglenook was given a playful treatment. The first landing was partitioned by an elaborate screen of carved trees with birds fluttering among their foliage and nests interwoven with their branches. From the landing a second flight of stairs gave access to the bedroom corridor, furnished with a glazed screen overlooking the hall from above. Baillie Scott also provided an alternative set of steps with a stone vaulted ceiling, narrow and winding as if they were stolen from a fairy-tale castle, to connect the landing with the enclosed chamber above the inglenook. This miniature room was designed with windows overlooking the garden and the lake beyond it, and featured a second screen of carved trees framing a pair of interior unglazed windows that looked down onto the hall.

The fanciful elements in Baillie Scott's designs were inseparable from his romantic vision of domestic life which remained consistent throughout his career. In an article for *The Studio*, published in 1894, he imagined the modern medieval hall in use and, although the accompanying plans and sketches describe "a lofty hall" within an "ideal suburban house," the poetic relationship he conjured up for his readers between the planning and decoration of the home and the life within it was equally applicable to Blackwell. "I should like to picture to you a musical evening in this hall. In the ingle, seated on the broad seats, a company of friends are gathered around the blazing wood fire on the wide brick hearth. . . .There is no glaring gas, but here and there lamps and candles throw a soft suffused light. Above in the gallery are the musicians, and the strains of a violin are heard to their best advantage, while the position of the player gives an air of mystery to the music."[28]

In Baillie Scott's houses, sentiment and nostalgia were skillfully employed as decoys and antidotes to daringly unconventional arrangements. The provision of billiard and music rooms in country houses was identified with a particular status. They were the turn-of-the-century equivalents to today's domestic swimming pool and, by incorporating them into more modestly scaled homes, Baillie Scott subverted social hierarchies. Moreover, by mixing these rooms together within a single "modern historical" space, he meddled with the conventions of sexual segregation. He atoned for these sins with a sophisticated decorative language that charmed and reassured his clients, integrating traditional references with sharp contemporary accents.

The hall at Blackwell is paneled in oak, and stags' heads and other sporting trophies originally decorated the double-height space. Leaded light windows ornamented with heraldic shields are set within square-cut stone frames. A door connecting the dining room with the billiard-playing end of the room reinforced the patriarchal associations of the great hall as a space for smoking and drinking after dinner. The open area in the center of the room, however, was originally furnished in drawing-room style with a sofa and upholstered chairs which could be gathered around the fire or pushed to the sides of the room for dances and banquets.[29] Between these masculine and feminine enclaves a refectory table at the very center of the room replaced the hall table. One early photograph shows it strewn with books and small vases of flowers, in keeping with drawing-room traditions, but it was styled to recall the enduring customs of the dining hall. "The family may or may not meet to talk or to study, but it is almost universally the custom to meet to eat. And so, to put the matter in another way, the central room may be obtained by an enlargement of the dining-room."[30]

These unorthodox and potentially alarming juxtapositions were made to work by the repetition of decorative motifs that linked the different parts of the room together and neutralized the distinctions between masculine and feminine domains. The mountain ash was chosen as a decorative theme throughout the house because it grew wild on the hills of the estate. Its berries and foliage were carved into the paneling and the timber brackets that frame the enclosure to the seat overlooking the billiard table; they recur in identical

RIGHT: Mountain ash foliage and berries, carved into the hall paneling.

form around the fireside inglenook. The motif reappears in less traditional form in wrought-iron fire dogs that Baillie Scott designed for the inglenook, and the same pattern of metal leaves "brightened by white enamelled flowers and scarlet berries" was incorporated into an immense electric light fitting suspended above the center of the room.

Baillie Scott was acutely aware of the emotional reactions that different colors and forms would provoke. Purple and blue were identified with spiritual superiority and a room decorated in these tones, he wrote, would be dainty and refined. Green was regarded as a "normal," satisfying color, and in Baillie Scott's decorative schemes it was used to counterbalance the base effects of incidental passages of yellow, orange, and red, which were believed to appeal to "animal instincts."[31] As a consequence, blue tulips decorate the stained-glass screen between the hall and the corridor, and the billiard-room recess was furnished with a frieze of blue peacocks parading before a predominantly green background of briar roses.[32]

The hall at Blackwell was not a "complete" interior. It was furnished by the clients with an assortment of pieces, but visitors to the Royal Academy in 1900 could view a watercolor perspective of the interior as it might have been.[33] The billiard table was carved with leaves and berries to match the inglenook and lit by an extroller with delicate, heart-motif shades. A frieze depicting maidens gathered beneath the boughs of the ubiquitous mountain ash concluded the feminine presence in this game-playing part of the room, and a winged armchair, covered with a loose patterned cover was drawn toward the inglenook fireplace.

Baillie Scott's prettily detailed perspectives and his persuasive philosophy, first published in *The Studio* and expanded in his book *Houses and Gardens* (published in 1906), were more influential than his actual interiors in disseminating the ideal of the living hall as a model for modern living. His watercolors often featured a corner of a room with no indication of scale so that they were equally appealing to clients who wanted to build a modest country retreat around a single multipurpose space and to more affluent homeowners, such as the Beresford Potters who commissioned Baillie Scott to add a new music room to their Elizabethan country house, Rake Manor in Surrey. It was in scaled-down versions, however, that Baillie Scott's propositions acquired their most radical implications.

By providing a generous internal porch, even in small suburban houses, he disposed of the problems of drafts and outdoor clothes, and the hall became the principal living space at the heart of the artistic house. The tradition of dividing the ground floor into cramped private spaces where the family actually lived and a "best parlour," which was kept for show, was swept aside, and the narrow passage hall with its role as a social sorting office was abolished. In his own house (the Red House, designed between 1892 and 1893) and in "A Small Country House" (designed for *The Studio* in 1898), Baillie Scott opened almost the entire ground floor into the hall using sliding partitions which could be closed to resemble paneling and to separate drawing-room and dining-room spaces. In 1900 he suggested that instead of planning the house as a series of rectangular boxes that squashed a large family into a series of

LEFT: Falkewood, one of the romantic interiors which Baillie Scott idealized in his book, *Houses and Gardens*, 1906.

RIGHT: 48 Storey's Way, Cambridge. Spaces open directly into one another to create an impression of breadth and a practical versatility in Baillie Scott's smaller houses.

small rooms, the drawing room and dining room could be reduced to appendages "not pretending to compete with it [the hall] as rooms, but rather becoming merely recesses"—similar to the chapels in a cathedral.[34] A "refectory" recess was arranged on one side of the hall, set apart for meals, and a similar "ladies' bower" was provided "for tea and music. . .characterized by a certain daintiness of treatment which bears a feminine relation to the masculine ruggedness of the hall. Viewed from the great bench of the hall ingle, it appears as some delicate and dainty Early English Lady Chapel seen through the massive pillars of a Norman nave."[35]

The imagery and language that Baillie Scott used to describe his domestic reforms disguises the controversial social implications of bringing men, women, and children together within a single space for most of the day, and he was at pains to quote Carlyle and Ruskin in defense of the respectability of "unassuming simplicity" in the English home. "More than this," cited Ruskin, "few shall seek."[36] His watercolors fuse the finishes and furnishings of the traditional hall with the decorative refinement of the drawing room. The settle and chairs which Muthesius described as indispensable to the hall were built into the ingle and mixed with more comfortable seats round the hearth as a gathering rather than a waiting place. The importance of good lighting became a vehicle for extravagant electric light fittings, and Muthesius's insistence on the "never-failing finishing touch of. . .the tall longcase clock of ancient memory," which was to be found, he believed, in antique form in every English hall, was presented in miniature in the form of a tall mantel clock.[37] Curtains and portières were used to cover doors and to screen staircase enclosures, and Baillie Scott's genius for color and pattern signaled earthy and esoteric areas within the room.

The success of the living hall as a key interior within the modern house was the most significant and the most surreptitious factor in undermining Victorian domestic

conventions and establishing the character of the Arts and Crafts home. Muthesius noted that "once a hall has gained the favor of the occupants of a house, the drawing-room is doomed"; ultimately the living hall became the living room.[38] In bungalows, designer cottages, and country houses, an insistence that the hall "should receive its guests with composure and dignity, but still with brightness, open arms and warmth" transformed even the smallest hall into a comfortable room.[39] An Arts and Crafts commitment to "honest simplicity"—along with the philosophy that every detail of the house from the path to the front door to the design of the cutlery should be conceived and constructed to the same artistic standard—overruled Victorian scruples about opening the front door almost directly into a living space.

In smaller houses such as Hollybank, designed by Voysey in 1903, and 48 Storey's Way, designed by Baillie Scott in 1912, the process of arrival, built up between the front gate and covered porch through a succession of refined cottage details and surface textures, was perfectly fulfilled by the revelation of a single living space dominating the ground floor plan. The continuity of materials throughout the house contributed to an effect of breadth and repose which belied the small scale of these houses.

Despite its candor, the Arts and Crafts hall remained susceptible to a Victorian determination that the hall should create an impression. It was concerned with artistic rather than material display, however, and its most impressive features could be justified as utilitarian. The restrained colors of a Macintosh pendant lamp coupled with the elongated lines of a stylized chimneypiece and the uncompromising geometry of a gridded front door, nevertheless, were designed with an austerity and an assertiveness which would have qualified, at the turn of the century, as a form of creative intimidation.

"AT HOME" IN THE DRAWING ROOM

HE VICTORIAN DRAWING ROOM, more than any other room in the house, was a reflection of the personal style and interests of its mistress. Her sense of dress and decorum determined its decoration, and the room was furnished and arranged to serve her requirements as a hostess. Apart from business associates, who were received in the library, visitors were welcomed from the hall into the drawing room, and the design of the room and its contents were tailored to meet the social conventions of entertaining. The idealization of women in late Victorian culture as angelic figures representing spiritual purity contrasted sharply with women's claims to political and professional independence outside the home, and such contrasts are visible in the decorative identities of different drawing-room styles within the Arts and Crafts Movement. In some artistic and intellectual circles, the concept of a distinctive feminine domain at the social heart of the home was dispensed with entirely. In others it was accentuated in esoteric white interiors which renounced the practical considerations and compromises of the commercial world.

The act of decorating the drawing room as a demonstration of personal identity and as an essential scene-setting exercise to establish the character of the home as a social space is epitomized in Margaret Oliphant's novel *Miss Marjoribanks*. The heroine, Lucilla, claims control of her widower father's house as soon as she comes of age by redecorating and furnishing the first-floor drawing room in colors that will complement her complexion. Although Lucilla's sole ambition was ostensibly "to be a comfort to dear papa," the restyling of the room was the first step in her grand design to establish a salon—based in the provincial town, where her father was a doctor—over which she would reign supreme. Every Thursday at nine the "enchanted chamber" of the drawing room provided a backdrop for carefully orchestrated "Evenings" which Lucilla designed to transform "the chaotic elements of society. . .into one grand unity."[1]

Lucilla's capacity as a hostess—her raison d'être—extended to every detail of the occasion. She selected the guests, choreographed their groupings, and, by letting it be known that unmarried maidens like herself should dress in the simple white "high" muslin gowns idealized by James McNeill Whistler in his paintings of young virgin women, she even prescribed the costumes. Married women were permitted more extravagant and revealing gowns. By coordinating appearances, Lucilla established a decorative language of refinement that dictated a standard for conversation and behavior at her gatherings. The design of the drawing room and the arrangement of the furniture became cues and props or psychological pointers in Lucilla's master plan.

Oliphant's novels were immensely popular during the second half of the nineteenth century, not least because of the pleasure and sensitivity with which she portrayed the minutiae of ordinary feminine interests. Her representation of the home as a dramatic setting was reiterated by other novelists and painters of the period. Her heroines delighted in the textures and technicalities of needlework, and they excelled in the manipulation of social gatherings. Lucilla's Thursday "Evenings" were typical of the "At Homes" which Muthesius records as an immutable convention occurring at nine in the evenings. The nature of these "At Homes" ranged from exclusive artistic salons, which were a vital component in the social apparatus of patronage, to simple rural get-togethers which depended for their success on moonlight: guests would not attend unless they could be sure of finding their way safely home again. Henry James placed his female characters "At Home" when they were engaged in complex social maneuvering, whereas in Oliphant's novels the process of bringing all the disparate elements into play and the social implications of every detail of the occasion are the substance of the plot.

No written invitations were issued for the "At Home" and Lucilla was careful to distinguish her regular "Evenings" from occasional parties and more formal musical evenings—where professional players were paid to perform and the guests were required to be quiet and listen. The drawing room was furnished with a piano so that Lucilla and her friends might sing and play to the assembled company, but lengthy renditions were reserved for fine summer evenings when chairs were set out under the plane tree in the garden and the drawing-room windows were opened to allow the music to drift outside. "You know I never would consent to be too musical when everybody was in one room," Lucilla confessed to one of her aristocratic mentors. "It does not

matter so much, when there are a suite; but then papa, you know, is only a professional man, and I have but one drawing-room." [2]

The piano was a vehicle for rampant flirtations and romantic seductions. Women of a marriageable age selected their music with intent and directed their attentions toward particular suitors who stood by the piano to admire them. Sexually provocative behavior that would have been potentially scandalous elsewhere in the house was condoned within the social structure of the drawing room. Lucilla instructed an eligible bachelor to flirt indiscriminately in the middle of the room but when he succumbed to the charms of the drawing master's daughter "still crimson and splendid, triumphing over her limp dress and all her disadvantages, by the piano," and spent an unseemly amount of time downstairs with her (to fetch a cup of tea) he sustained the disapproval of the entire company. [3]

The piano was also played at more casual, afternoon gatherings in the drawing room. May Morris recalled how the artist Kate Faulkner would sit at "a dear little square piano" in her long drawing room overlooking Queen Square, surrounded by Morris furniture and Burne-Jones drawings, and sing songs from the *Echos du Temps Passé*.[4] Little girls learned the piano as a social grace. Mary Gamble, for example, learned to sing and play the piano as a very young child together with drawing, knitting, sewing patchwork blocks, and making paper flowers. She took lessons in French but "music was a part of her daily life from her mother."[5] Muthesius observed with some dismay that although the English were the most unmusical race in the world, a grand piano was to be found in every drawing room; he also noted that the upright piano was an object of contempt, associated either with impermanence or impoverishment.[6] The presence of a Bechstein grand, however, did not necessarily signify any musical accomplishment: "Even among the educated there is a lack of critical judgement of quality in music that would be impossible in any other country."[7]

Initially, attempts by Arts and Crafts designers to integrate the piano into the overall composition of the drawing room were limited to superficial decorations. Morris and Burne-Jones initiated a trend for painted and inlaid grand piano cases which was perpetuated by artists like Louise Powell. A more far-reaching ambition to rid the upright or "cottage" piano of its petty bourgeois associations and to accentuate its rustic simplicity was disparaged by Muthesius. "The mistake has been to consider a casing put together like a barn-door suitable to a delicate mechanism like that of the modern piano."[8] The problem, as one critic put it, "of making a household pet out of an elephant" was resolved by building a case around the projecting keyboard of the upright piano which could then be decorated in a manner which was both elegant and appropriate to the artistic drawing room.[9] Baillie Scott's "Manxman" design, exhibited in the London Arts and Crafts Exhibition of 1896, presented a new model for the artistic treatment of the piano. Its compact and versatile case fitted comfortably into the smaller drawing room or the living hall and, when it was not in use, it could be folded neatly away. The prototype was simply cased in green-stained oak with art metal hinges, but as the form increased in popularity and other designers and manufacturers adopted the idea of the piano as a "treasure chest" or sacred cabinet, an element of ceremony, appropriate to the social significance of the object, crept into the design of more elaborate cases. Pianos that were relatively demure when closed revealed elaborate flowers, fruiting trees, and other feminine motifs inlaid in colored woods, mother-of-pearl, and jewel-like enamels when they were opened to be played.[10]

The evening "At Home" in the drawing room often followed a more select dinner, presided over by the man of the house and dominated by his guests. There was a deliberate juxtaposition, as Lucilla complained, between the patriarchal proceedings of the dining room—"Papa has always some men to dinner. . .and it is so dreadfully slow for me with a heap of men"—and the etiquette of the drawing room where the men were bossed and cajoled by the hostess.[11] A creative partnership, in many households, insured that the combination of serious discussions over dinner followed by adroit introductions and discreet flirtations in the drawing room were put to great effect. In Lucilla's case, however, the dinners were tolerated with a sense of duty while her father escaped to the library after the briefest appearance in the drawing room. There was an acceptance, too, that although the decoration of the drawing room should create an aesthetic environment for Lucilla's "Evenings," the library and dining room were beyond the powers of feminine influence.

The hall, the dining room, and the drawing room were designed to function as a suite of rooms during the "At Home." When Lucilla and her father's guests ascended the stairs after dinner to join the larger party already assembled in the drawing room, they left the masculine domain for the feminine realm and conversations and codes of behavior were expected to lift accordingly. "It is a generally accepted rule that, as in the dining-room everything should be heavy and sombre, so the drawing-room should exhibit a light and airy appearance befitting the purpose for which it is ordained."[12] Pale colors and more delicate fabrics and furniture distinguished the decoration of the room; in many Victorian houses white was considered an unsuitable color for the hall because it detracted from the sense of deferred gratification when the door to the drawing room was opened. The hall paneling at Standen, for example, was originally painted red in contrast to the white paneling in the drawing room.[13]

In addition to the evening gatherings, more intimate "At Homes" were held in the drawing room between three and six in the afternoon, when women paid calls on one another. Men were generally excluded from these occasions, as it was assumed that they were at work, although Saturday "At Homes" were popular with gentlemen. They were also "privileged to call on Sunday, after church, and on Sunday evenings."[14] On weekdays a married woman would leave her husband's card in the hall as well as her own, as a token presence. Women were advised to assign one day each week to the reception of visitors, dealing with tradespeople in the mornings and letting it be known that they would be at home to social callers in the afternoons. On these occasions the drawing room became a regular meeting place for established circles of friends. "Afternoon tea is now made an excuse for the readings, musicals, and literary réunions so fashionable in New York; but for this purpose ladies are summoned earlier in the afternoon, and tea is served later."[15] It was also "a convenient alias for flirtation" as the novels of Henry James describe, where gossip was exchanged and romantic engagements were plotted or unraveled.[16] The "five o'clock tea" which began in England and rapidly spread to America was advocated in one etiquette manual as a method of entertaining convenient for a lady's servants and inexpensive for her husband.[17] It generated new fashions in plain, high-necked "tea gowns," as well as "tea tables" with flaps forming shelves on each side on which to put plates, cups, and saucers.

Simple refreshments, which Muthesius described as "positively inadequate" by German standards, provided a ceremonial focus for these gatherings.[18] Bread and butter, cakes, and biscuits were offered, and marriageable daughters were brought down from the nursery and permitted to make the tea as a prelude to courtship rituals: "The sight of a pretty girl making tea is always so dear to the masculine heart."[19] In James's *The Portrait of a Lady*, Pansy Osmond was positioned at a table making tea as "a dear little maid" at her stepmother's "At Home." Although the intention was to introduce her to the English lord whom her father wanted her to marry, it was into the "aromatic depths" of the teapot that she secretly pledged her love for another suitor of whom he disapproved.[20] Nanda, the heroine in James' *The Awkward Age,* confessed that she usually took her tea in the nursery: "They bring it up in a cup, all made and very weak, with a piece of bread-and-butter in the saucer. That's because I'm so young."[21] In a plot which dealt precisely with the gray area between conventional good manners and a nonchalant disregard for old-fashioned standards that marked the modern age, Nanda was taught by her mother "about the little things to do" so that she could "make tea beautifully." She was then dispatched to the apartment of an eligible bachelor with only an older unmarried man as a hopelessly inadequate but extremely wealthy chaperone in a calculated attempt to win the affections of the former and to provoke the latter into becoming her benefactor.

Servants were on hand at larger gatherings, but most women preferred to have a spirit lamp with a copper or silver kettle and a water pitcher close to the fireside so that the conversations at their "At Homes" need not be cramped by the presence of minions. A gentleman would "spring to the hostess's aid" in handing round the tea and cakes.[22] The tea things, stacked on a silver or wooden tray with two handles, were brought in by a maid and set on a low table close to the fire. The tea was poured by the mistress of the house or her daughter, however, and their implements were designed accordingly. Elegant water pitchers and teapots were designed as ceremonial objects, crafted in fine materials and ornamented to chime with the hostess' dress and jewelry. Ashbee's jeweled silver teapots and sugar bowls translated the opulence and individuality of his jewelry designs into domestic objects conceived as emblems of sexual maturity and authority. The fireside kettle, by comparison, was more closely identified with the hearth and its accoutrements. Voysey designed a spirit kettle and stand as a companion to the fire irons and screens which he devised as functional architectural ornaments.[23] By the turn of the century, electric kettles were recommended for the drawing rooms of progressive hostesses who were put off by "the horrible odour" of the spirit kettle, but these newfangled appliances were generally limited to the kitchen.[24]

Whether the drawing room was on the first floor of a town house or looking out across the garden of a suburban or country house, it was planned to cater to different social occasions. The furniture was arranged in small groups which were conducive to intimate conversations and to musical interludes—when the piano might briefly focus the attention of the entire room. There was no single focus, however, and the fireplace, the piano, and the bay window alternated as centers of attention. Although the drawing room was the family space for reading, chatting, and playing games, it was not used in the mornings and the orientation of the room was arranged to take advantage of the afternoon and evening sunlight. Individual callers were received from lunchtime onward and a sofa or upholstered settle was arranged close to the fire, together with comfortable armchairs, for these occasions.[25]

Arts and Crafts hostesses and their designers were acutely aware of the body language encouraged by different styles of chairs. "Soft-cheeked monstrosities upholstered all over" were positioned by the fireside because they supported the body "in a really refined

LEFT: An idealized image of the drawing room at The Pastures, designed by Voysey in 1901 with every item of furniture, even the ornaments on the mantel shelf, conforming to an architectural vision.

manner. . .for contemplation and day-dreaming."[26] Lucilla occasionally lay back in her chair "with that air of languor which so many young ladies excel in"[27] and which artists like Leighton and Moore immortalized in paint: "Her hand hung over the arm of her chair as if there was no longer any force in it. Her head fell back, her eyes were half closed."[28] Less comfortable wooden settees with loose upholstered seats and backs, and Queen Anne sofas with compact rectangular frames and tapered wooden legs, "positively not meant for reclining," were more useful on social occasions; their simple structures also appealed to architectural tastes.[29] In fact, the Arts and Crafts Movement coincided with a fashion for eighteenth-century furniture, and although Rhoda and Agnes Garrett complained of the "solicitous wrigglings" of chairs with fancy legs, there was a deliberate emphasis on variety in many drawing rooms to offer guests a selection of furniture.[30] They might present a magisterial or intimate image according to their choice of chair.

If there was a bay window in the drawing room it was often furnished with built-in seats. During the summer, when a decorative screen masked the unlit fire, the window became a setting for embroidery and other fine work requiring good natural light. There was a vogue for "cozy-corners," constructed around the fire or the window featuring a low wooden corner seat covered with flat, loose cushions and framed on two or three sides by a simple paneled structure or a fabric screen. In some instances the seat was secluded by hangings that could be "withdrawn should the occupant of the window seat desire to converse with anybody in the room."[31]

The House magazine recommended that in the smaller drawing room, a large easy chair should be grouped with several smaller chairs close to the piano, so that the hostess could recline while receiving her afternoon visitors, "and in the evening it can be turned round for the occupant to listen to the music."[32] Chintz covers patterned to Morris's designs or those of a younger generation of Arts and Crafts designers replaced the heavy wool and velvet upholstery fabrics favored in earlier drawing rooms. Used as loose covers or to reupholster favorite chairs and sofas, they helped to bind the necessary assortment of furniture together and, because they were washable, they were promoted for their healthy and hygienic qualities. "Thus the whole drawing-room has gradually been transformed into a room decorated in chintz. . .The clean chintz covers and matching curtains give the room an air of freshness, healthfulness and fragrance. One feels the same confidence in it as in a freshly made bed."[33]

The feminine identity of the drawing room and the inevitable confusion of its distinct groupings—exacerbated by incidental chairs and tables which were moved to meet the needs of different social occasions—was a subject of derision among Arts and Crafts architects. Muthesius, who trained as an architect, complained that the insistence on prettiness, casualness, and superficiality which made it agreeable to chat and linger in the drawing room was disastrous in terms of style. Elegance, he wrote was "usually combined with caprice and that love of frippery and knick-knacks by the thousand that characterises the modern English society woman."[34] Even the most cluttered Arts and Crafts drawing room, however, in which, as one popular song put it "You have to go in and out pickapack," was widely recognized as an improvement upon the dark colors and heavy fabrics of earlier Victorian versions, where antimacassars were spread across plush furniture and every available surface was covered with images and ornaments.[35]

Progressive architects sought to rationalize and unify the disparate elements of the room by building the furniture into the interior and establishing a rhythm of decorative motifs which recurred in the fabrics and fittings as well as in the structural decoration of the room. The interior architecture was treated with a light simplicity. If there was paneling it was generally painted white, together with the joinery around the fireplace and window surrounds. The moldings were more delicate, accentuating the graceful, feminine character of the room, and the joinery often framed panels for fabric hangings. The frieze and ceiling, too, were invariably painted white, and structural beams were plastered and distempered rather than exposed. At Melsetter House in Orkney, Scotland, designed by W. R. Lethaby for Thomas and Theodosia Middlemore in 1898,

LEFT: The drawing room at Melsetter House, designed by W. R. Lethaby in 1898, viewed from the hall.

ABOVE: A high window lights the deep drawing-room bay at Melsetter in the late afternoon.

both the drawing room and the hall have white painted paneling, but in the drawing room its proportions and detailing are more refined, and French windows align with the double-doors from the hall so that they open to reveal a flood of light. The room is L-shaped with tall south- and west-facing windows lighting a deep bay so that the play of light throughout the afternoon contrasts with the darker, internal character of the hall and its monumental stone chimneypiece.

In Britain, when architects collaborated with artists and skilled craftsmen, the beams and friezes of the drawing room were sometimes decorated with ornamental plasterwork. A plaster frieze, called "Honesty," exhibited in the 1896 Arts and Crafts Exhibition by the sculptor George Frampton, found a permanent home in a house by his fellow Art Workers' Guild member Voysey, in Studland Bay, Dorset. The architect Ernest Gimson apprenticed himself to a firm, Whitcombe and Priestley, to learn to mold and model plaster "in the old way."[36] "Mr Whitcombe was puzzled by Gimson's 'messing about with plaster, dirty stuff,' but finally explained it as 'just his hobby.'"[37] Because of his friendships with Ernest Barnsley and W. R. Lethaby and in a spirit of shared enthusiasm for a forgotten art, Gimson patterned the plaster beams at Barnsley's cottage at Sapperton and he decorated Lethaby's first commission for a house, Avon Tyrrel, in Hampshire. Lethaby described the meandering patterns of Gimson's early friezes, depicting roses, pinks, honeysuckle, and strawberry plants drawn from nature, as "easy, masterly and just right, quite original and modern, but as good, every bit, as 'old work' and yet simple as piecrust."[38] The plaster molds for the drawing and dining rooms at Melsetter are also thought to have been by Gimson.

Manufacturers such as Anaglypta and Lincrusta produced relief wallpapers and fibrous plaster panels so that more derivative drawing rooms could enjoy the appearance of original plaster friezes. Although there were elitist concerns about the integrity of these prefabricated effects, fashionable architects, including Voysey and

LEFT AND RIGHT: Architects revived the traditional craft of ornamental plasterwork in English country houses. A simple pattern of pinks at Melsetter (left) is attributed to Ernest Gimson while the swirling berries and foliage of the mountain ash in the elegant drawing room at Blackwell were designed by Baillie Scott and installed in prefabricated panels.

Baillie Scott, supplied the manufacturers with designs. Baillie Scott used fibrous plaster panels made to his own designs for the drawing-room frieze at Blackwell because, apart from being much cheaper than hand work, the panels could be applied quickly without bringing the damp and mess of fresh plaster into the house.[39] The swirling plaster leaves and berries of the mountain ash are gracefully attenuated by comparison with their robust counterparts carved into oak and stone in the hall. Baillie Scott was able to exaggerate the feminine qualities of the white drawing room at Blackwell because the more communal, family requirements of the space had been transferred to the living hall.

At Standen, too, the piano and the rituals of afternoon tea took place in the living hall so that when Webb visited the Beales in January 1898 he found eleven people gathered around the fireplace for tea. As a consequence of its success Webb made the hall larger and lighter. The paneling was repainted in white and the architect extended the room northward, writing to his clients with a characteristic attention to every detail that the "tea-table could then be put opposite the fireplace, and the piano—which at present rather cuts the room in two, could very well go into the new projection."[40] The combination of the hall and drawing room gave Standen, and other country houses of its type, the advantages of a suite of rooms for entertaining, which previously only much larger country houses had enjoyed. In winter, when the large windows that characterized the light and airy drawing room made it difficult to keep warm, the room could be left unheated and unused.[41]

As Standen was a country retreat, the drawing room was used more for family gatherings than for entertaining, but the conventions of the period still prevailed. Only flower arrangers and servants entered the drawing room in the mornings. Margaret Beale and her daughters read the papers, wrote letters, and consulted over embroidery colors and patterns in the morning room and "no novels" were permitted until after lunch.[42] When they retired to the drawing room in the afternoons, Margaret would read aloud, knitting socks throughout, while her daughters and grandchildren embroidered and sketched one another. Margaret was an expert needlewoman, and the decorative highlight of the drawing room was a pair of silk embroidered hangings to either side of the fireplace, designed by Morris, which she and her daughters completed around 1896.[43] The decoration of the room reflected Margaret's artistic taste but it also offers a rare insight into the way that Arts and Crafts designers would negotiate and develop interiors in collaboration with their clients through a sequence of distinct stages, often over a period of several years.

Webb's careful relationships with his clients ensured that he continued to be actively involved in the decoration and furnishing of his buildings for many years after his initial engagement as an architect. Standen was completed in August 1894 but Webb's site book for the following April outlines a visit after the new building had had time to settle and dry out in order to discuss the final color schemes and the choice of wallpapers. His involvement as a partner of Morris & Co. gave him an intimate knowledge of their patterns and furniture. He had drawn the birds onto Morris's design for the "Trellis" paper. Thus, when it was specified for the corridor next to the conservatory at Standen, he fixed the vine eyes so that the plants in the conservatory would grow across the circular windows and appear, from the other side of the wall, to extend the wallpaper

ABOVE: Detail of the "Artichoke" hanging embroidered by Mrs. Beale and her daughters to a pattern designed by Morris.

RIGHT: Upholstered armchairs from Morris & Co., drawn around the fireside at Standen by the light of a Benson standard lamp. The "Artichoke" embroidery was originally hung on either side of the fireplace.

pattern. He was by no means bound to Morris & Co. as a supplier, though, and on several occasions he accompanied his women clients on shopping expeditions to buy furnishings and fabrics from other sources for his interiors.[44]

The furniture for Standen was a mixture of pieces that the Beales brought down from their London home and new pieces purchased from Morris & Co. and other sources. Morris & Co.'s Connaught easy chairs were upholstered in the same Utrecht Velvet as the Morris Chippendale double settee, which catered to a taste for eighteenth-century furniture. There were no "solicitous wriggling" legs, however: Margaret Beale's cousins included Rhoda and Agnes Garrett, and a copy of their *Suggestions for House Decoration* was to be found on the Standen bookshelves. She probably bought a second settee made to their designs independently of Webb, but the complete furnishing of the drawing room cannot be reconstructed. The smaller pieces of furniture, including Morris's Sussex chairs, were relegated to the servants' quarters or given away as they fell from fashion over successive generations.[45]

Webb was adept at making his clients believe that his conception of the interior and its furnishings matched their own and, although the interior architecture of the Beales' drawing room and its decoration were assembled gradually, they conform to a single vision. The room faces south and tall windows with seats built into the recesses make it one of the lightest as well as the largest rooms in the house. Webb provided a deep south-facing bay, extending the fireplace wall, a place where Margaret and her daughters could knit and embroider, protected from the glare of the sun by a projecting canopy outside. A simple stone fireplace is set within a timber frame almost flush with the plane of the wall because, as Muthesius observed, "during afternoon visits quite a large company may need to cluster round the fire," making the more intimate recessed fireplace bay inappropriate. A large mirror or a painting was habitually hung above the drawing-room fireplace and, in more elaborate Arts and Crafts designs, the architecture of the chimneypiece was designed to frame a specially commissioned painting or gesso panel. In Webb's chimneypiece at Standen, a pattern of white-painted panels delineates the form and proportions of a substantial fireplace in a witty abbreviation; the space above is filled by an abstract geometric pattern of paneling.

Muthesius described the importance of a dado shelf and a generous mantelpiece in the drawing room, often flanked by little shelves: "The guiding principle will always be to create as much room as possible for small ornaments."[46] Webb designed a pair of slender shelves to flank the fireplace at Standen, but the elegantly profiled moldings

LEFT: Morris & Co. produced eighteenth-century style furniture from the 1880s to cater for clients with more conservative tastes. This mahogany Chippendale double settee was chosen by the Beales for the drawing room at Standen. It is flanked by Morris Rose chintz curtains to the conservatory doors, but the curtains to the windows in the south wall are patterned with Morris's "Sunflower" design. The chalk drawing is by Burne-Jones.

ABOVE: Armchair and corner-cabinet in the morning room, designed by Rhoda and Agnes Garrett.

which he designed in place of a mantel shelf and as a picture rail precluded any possibility of a clutter of ornaments. The drawing room, nevertheless, was the most important room in the house for the display of precious objects. It was described as "the jewel casket of the house" and the "real centre of attraction." The largest piece of furniture in the room was invariably a glazed cabinet, placed against the long wall between the door and the fireplace for the display of the most valuable china and other fine pieces.[47]

Instead of paneling the room throughout, Webb introduced passages of Morris & Co. wallpaper to tone with the colors in the upholstered furniture. Although the "Sunflower" wallpaper was not ordered until 1895, after the building had fully settled, it reiterated a motif that he had already introduced into the architectural ornament of the room in the form of copper repoussé cheeks to the fireplace, patterned with intertwining sunflowers. He had taken them with him to a site visit in July 1894, during the final stage of the building work, leaving them for the Beales to approve, and it was at this stage that sunflower wall sconces were proposed as a solution to the question of electric lighting. He wrote to Margaret Beale: "I carefully considered as to what might be done for the electric lights in the drawing-room, and concluded that embossed copper sconces standing on the picture rail (of the same kind of work as to the fireplace plates) would be the best form for the finish of these bracket supports—something like this sketch."[48] Six sconces were made for the room by the metalworker John Pearson; Webb's respect for the creative integrity of the craftsman allowed that each one should be slightly different. With characteristic precision he made a note to Mrs. Beale, however, that "The copper plates should not be scoured, but only occasionally rubbed with wash leather."[49]

Electric light fittings were the quintessence of modernity in the 1890s and early 1900s, and they were used by Arts and Crafts designers and their clients to define the separate areas within the drawing room. Webb's design for wall sconces adapted a form invented to reflect the light of candles and had been well suited, subsequently, to concealing the pipes to gas lighting fixtures. The translucent flower shade, however, and the spirals of colored glass twisted around the flex to Webb's lamps accentuated the cleanliness and simplicity of electricity. Elsewhere in the house, slender pendant light fittings designed by W.A.S. Benson with opalescent glass shades also depended for their effect upon the luxury of "the new wire-conveyed spark."[50] Benson, who became managing director of Morris & Co. in 1896, produced a range of affordable electric light fittings assembled from standard tubular brass and copper components, and his table

and standard lamps introduced a new flexibility to the lighting of the drawing room. Although a good general light was considered essential to the success of evening entertainments, Standen was typical of Arts and Crafts houses in its use of small movable table lamps and standard lamps to create an atmosphere of intimacy around the fireside.

In the drawing room of the Gamble House in Pasadena, the electric light fittings are the final element in an interior so meticulously planned that even the position and size of the rugs on the floor were preordained. Three rectangular pendant lamps, designed by Greene and Greene, are aligned across the center of the room, but the middle lamp is longer, proportioned in response to the cruciform plan of the space. A wide window bay faces westward to catch the afternoon sun and, on the opposite side of the room, is mirrored by an inglenook with smaller lanterns suspended from massive Burma teak beams, which frame and define this wide recess.

The colors and materials of the Gamble House drawing room illustrate the demise of the feminine "throne room" because it was subjected to an architectural concept of the house as a complete work of art. Mary Gamble was actively involved, nevertheless, in every aspect of the furnishing of the room. A hasty sketch of the pendant living-room lights on a page torn from Charles Greene's notebook suggests that they were drawn on the spot in consultation with Mary during a site visit.[51] On another page a sketch of one of the inglenook "lamp-lanterns" is annotated, "Soft light but bright. . .for reading over seat for Mr G.," and a note on the color for the hall frieze—"brownish—not to [sic] monotonous"—suggests the client's voice rather than that of the architect.[52] Mary Gamble kept a workbook in which the items of furniture commissioned from the Greenes and their cost were recorded. Slight disparities between the interior elevations of the drawing room and the final arrangement of the furniture also indicate a close working relationship between the client and her architect throughout the planning of the house.[53] Although all the components of the conventional Arts and Crafts drawing room are in place at the Gamble House, however, the frivolous and haphazard identity of the room has been rationalized away. Mary Gamble was a strict Presbyterian and frivolity was perhaps not her style, but whatever the drawing room lacked in pretty patterns and pale colors was recompensed by the utility and dignity of the arrangement of the room and the sense that it was fully integrated within the complete house.

The walls are paneled with the same Burma teak as the hall, and a carved redwood frieze depicting mountains refers to the house's position on the edge of the Arroyo Seco and to the social importance of the room. All of the furniture in the drawing room was designed by the Greenes and their drawings, together with early photographs, describe a coordinated approach to the layout and furnishing of the room. No lolling or lounging would have been sanctioned on the long timber-framed settee, proportioned to complement the window bay. An occasional table and an elegant upright chair were also set within the bay, and the group was closed by a larger table and two chairs, positioned toward the middle of the room so that larger groups could gather in the bay at tea time. The window bay was designed to be used in the afternoons and early evenings when the sun, moving around to the west of the house, lights the entire room, but a Tiffany table

ABOVE: Electric light fittings were designed to define the separate spaces within the Gamble House drawing room. Three pendant lamps (left) across the center of the room were supplemented by lanterns (right) suspended over the fireplace bay.

lamp was prominently displayed on the large table for ornamental as well as practical purposes. "In the reception or living rooms of a modern house no object of furnishing so quickly attracts the eye and forcibly impresses the visitor with its presence as the movable reading lamp. . .Its very prominence. . .tends to give to the visitor the keynote of the taste of him or her who is responsible for the room."[54] The Tiffany lamp was an instance of Mary Gamble's taste as a collector but her fine collection of Rookwood pottery, paradoxically, was exhibited in the privacy of the master bedroom. Although cabinets were built in to either side of the drawing-room fireplace, they were fitted with art glass so that their contents did not distract from the harmony of the interior. The room itself, rather than one or two of its ornaments, was intended for display.

The noble expression of load-bearing timbers exquisitely formed and finished which distinguishes the hall at the Gamble House is manifest in monumental teak trusses that curve down from queenposts to frame the window and fireplace recesses in the drawing room. The inglenook is emphatically wide to echo the proportions of the opposite bay; consequently, the built-in bench seats are too far apart for conversations to be held easily across the fire. Each bench, however, capable of seating three in a line, if not in comfort (these are hard, straight-backed benches), and there is room in front of the fire for a pair of Greene and Greene rocking chairs to be pulled forward into the inglenook. On cold days and in the evenings, Mary Gamble would have served the tea or coffee at a low table in the inglenook where smaller, marble-topped tables were provided for the convenience of her family and guests. Gray-green Grueby or Rookwood tiles surround the hearth, inset with a pattern of undulating stems and stylized flowers which glitter as they reflect the afternoon sun.[55]

Mary Gamble was actively engaged in church and charitable work, and it is hard to imagine her upright piano as an instrument for improper provocations. The case was designed by Greene and Greene to blend with the paneling in the very corner of the room, and it was positioned so that its music should be heard with equal clarity in the adjoining living hall. There was some controversy over the propriety of building bookshelves into a room where serious subjects of conversation were supposedly banished: in more conservative drawing rooms, a compromise was achieved in the form of low, revolving bookstands with shelves below a tabletop.[56] At the Gamble House, however, the serious nature of the drawing room and its occupants was left in no doubt by the provision of bookcases at the far end of the room; a small table was provided for reading or games.

The term "drawing room," which derived from the practice of withdrawing after dinner, was seldom used in America. In both large and small houses a "living room" indicated a more family-oriented and inclusive approach to the space and a "parlor" suggested a cozy room in the smaller house. As the ideal of the living hall revolutionized the planning of bungalows and cottages in Britain and America, the characteristics of the living room and the hall were combined, so that in Craftsman houses and bungalows, issues of gender and the finer points of etiquette were superseded by a more utilitarian approach to living. To some extent, there was a two-way influence between these smaller houses and buildings like the Gamble House in which the decorative treatment of the drawing or living room can barely be distinguished from that of the more masculine rooms of the house. The traditional features—the prominent fireplace, the window bay, and the piano—were distilled to give form and meaning to more compact interiors in which the furniture was built-in. The ornament, aside, perhaps, from a Rookwood vase for flowers, was architectural or utilitarian.

The Craftsman promoted an image of the living room in soft, earth colors. Native redwood paneling, sturdy Stickley furniture, and ocher friezes and curtains, together with green upholstery fabric, were designed to suggest a rustic simplicity and a profound harmony with nature. Although the inclusion of an architect-designed piano, a window recess with built-in seat, and a table strewn with books and furnished with a Tiffany-style lamp referred specifically to drawing-room conventions, the flounces and knick-knacks, the delicate patterns and moldings that characterized the room as a feminine domain were modernized away, and the room was described as a place where men and women might work or relax.[57]

Ernest Batchelder and his wife Alice Coleman exemplified this creative and progressive mentality that *The Craftsman* set out to encourage. Batchelder, an artist and

ABOVE: A wide inglenook accentuates the shelter and warmth of the fireside in the Gamble House drawing room. It is balanced, on the opposite side of the room, by a window bay of the same proportions.

teacher, designed his own Pasadena bungalow (probably with the help of an architect) in 1909, and later wrote articles on design for *The Craftsman*. When the house was first envisaged, he was a bachelor and his workshop, later to become a factory producing decorative Arts and Crafts tiles, was in its infancy. The front door of his bungalow opens directly into a living room paneled in redwood, with exposed beams and timbers articulating the house's pitch roof. Redwood was one of the cheapest and most readily available materials for bungalow builders, but the common practice of concealing the wood beneath layers of stain and varnish was revoked by Arts and Crafts designers. Instead, its vigorous grain and soft surface texture "rubbed with a wax dressing to

RIGHT: Watercolor perspectives in *The Craftsman* reduced the essential components of the artistic drawing room—the window bay, the piano, the fireside and table for books—down to their most compact and affordable form.

preserve the natural colour" was exposed.[58] The candor and simplicity which marks the organization of the interior and its decoration was never crude, however. Wooden pegs articulate the construction of a tall frame of redwood uprights which enclose a window seat, giving the effect of a bay, and Batchelder initially intended to paint the living-room frieze with scenes from Chaucer's *Canterbury Tales*.[59]

The focus of the room is an immense brick fireplace tiled with Batchelder's own ceramics, which he is believed to have built as a wedding present to his fellow artist, the concert pianist Alice Coleman, whom he married in 1912. Symbols for their union, based on Donatello's "Murzoco," are worked into two ceramic panels at the top of the chimneypiece. On one side the figure holds a shield decorated with Batchelder's emblem, a rabbit, and on the other the shield contains a harp, perhaps referring to Alice's angelic qualities as well as her profession as a musician. The Viking ships which appear elsewhere in the design were a common turn-of-the-century symbol for a journey through life or a pilgrimage and the three pairs of birds which form the centerpiece to the design may have been allusions to nesting partners or to a spiritual union.[60]

For Alice, the Batchelder living room was a place where work and social responsibilities were inseparable. A writing desk and music cabinet were built into one corner of the room, and her piano, where lessons as well as recitals were given, was at the heart of progressive musical activity in Pasadena. In a determined effort to introduce chamber music to California she founded the Coleman Chamber Music

Association, and she campaigned for a new concert hall and museum. When the critic Gussie Packard Dubois was invited to tea by the newly completed fireside, he waxed lyrical about her piano in the midst of the room as well as "the lanterns of exquisite design and colouring," the art tiles, and the domestic comforts of the hearth. "Bellows and kettle looked so friendly, and now and then, for very restlessness, a little silence fell while the fire spoke for us in its leaping flames."[61] Alice, however, was quick to point out the potential of her own domestic situation as a model for public improvement. A new museum and art gallery, she persuaded him, would "bring the best in music and art within reach of all and develop the ability to make artistic homes and surroundings like these."[62]

No longer a space for withdrawing, a more direct relationship was cultivated between the Arts and Crafts living room and the world outside the home. Feminine activities which had been primarily amateur and domestic, from embroidery and music making to interior design, began to offer a means toward professional independence for women. Margaret Beale's daughter Maggie studied fine art in Paris and at the Slade in London, and May Morris's drawing room at 8 Hammersmith Terrace became the embroidery studio for Morris & Co. Several of the needlewomen who worked under her direction were related to her father's circle of friends: W. B. Yeats's sister Lily; Mary De Morgan, sister of the potter; and Mrs. Jack, who was married to Philip Webb's former assistant. The firm's chief furniture designer would have been welcome callers to her mother's "Sunday Afternoons" where embroidery was practiced as an accomplishment and a spectacle.

Jane Morris had reclined on her couch, "her long pale hands moving deftly over some rich embroidery," and when the occasion demanded, "there would come exciting moments when she would rise and fling the great portière down and spread it out."[63] In May's drawing room, however, women gathered to work—rather than to show off their long pale hands—and to stave off the indolence of protracted afternoons. Her artistic friends were joined by less privileged needlewomen who were recruited from the Royal School of Needlework and other schools, which fundamentally altered the social dynamics as well as the motivations of the women in attendance. May Morris's drawing room is an extreme example of the social changes, often accommodated with only minimal alterations to appearances, which affected women's lives in the decades around the turn of the century. Within a single generation the opportunities that women created for themselves altered the manner in which the drawing room was used as a social space. Although feminine discretion meant that fundamental changes in attitude were often concealed beneath a superficial compliance with conventions, reforms in the design of the drawing room represent some of the most subtle and socially revealing innovations in the Arts and Crafts home.

CHAPTER FIVE

DRESSING
FOR DINNER

LEFT: The dining room at Standen, with the laid table as the decorative focus of the room. Benson pendant lamps cast a pattern of rays across the ceiling.

INNER INVARIABLY TOOK PLACE at seven o'clock in the Arts and Crafts home. It was a long drawn-out occasion, often running to seven courses, and the formalities of the meal, the precision with which the table was laid—with a crisp white cloth and with glasses and cutlery lined up to denote the succession of courses—established a standard for the decoration and furnishing of the entire room. The set table was the central focus of the dining room: the positions of the doors and windows, the fireplace, and the sideboard were all planned as components in the rituals of service. Even in quite ordinary and relatively relaxed households, the evening meal was an occasion for ceremony. The family and their guests would assemble in the drawing room until the butler sounded the gong in the hall three times, when the gentlemen would escort the ladies in to dinner. Place settings were absolutely fixed. The master of the house sat at the head of the table opposite his wife, no matter how large the space between them loomed, and their children and guests were arranged in order of superiority down either side. In many marriages the evening meal was not exactly a meeting of minds, and readers of *The Ladies' Home Journal* were encouraged to keep it that way. "Never argue at the table but tell pleasant stories, relate or read anecdotes, and look out for the good of all."[1] The table, they were advised, was "a sort of domestic

altar" and the breaking of bread among the family was to be treated as "a joyful, almost sacramental meal." [2]

The table was a sacrificial offering in terms of time and creative expertise. Painstaking thought and exquisite taste were demanded of the mistress of the house in overseeing the arrangement of candles, glasses, and fine silver, and the strictest protocol catered to every detail in the presentation and service of the meal.[3] A thick cloth protected the tabletop from hot plates but it was also intended to absorb the harsh sounds of cutlery on plates and to soften the solid feel of the table. A white damask cloth was laid on top but silks and other fabrics that could not be washed were thought unsuitable for the dining room. "The proper place for silk and satin and painted chiffon and embroidery is the boudoir and the drawing-room; and the woman who puts such incongruities on her dining-table, either does so in imitation of someone else, without giving the matter a moment's personal thought, or else she is deficient in a fundamental sense of the fitness of things—in other words, lacks good taste." [4]

Plates were never laid out before the food was served because it was thought that "unwarmed plates would be useless and it would be inconvenient and pointless to put the soup-plates on them." [5] Instead beautiful plates were brought into play throughout the meal, so that "as the dinner progressed the guest revel[ed] in unexpected surprises," and every month *The House* published designs for "the table tasteful," explaining how to fold napkins into ingenious shapes.[6] Quantities of flowers were usually arranged by the mistress of the house in silver or crystal bowls which stood on the runner, and more delicate blooms were strewn in a pattern across the cloth. Single stems, gracefully arranged in small vases around the table, were preferred to a tall centerpiece because the pendant lamp in the dining room was often hung low over the center of the table, plus it was bad form to arrange flowers so that the diners could not see one another's faces.

Although the Arts and Crafts Movement demanded a reduction of ornament, it coincided with a marked increase in the use of fresh flowers to decorate the home. At Standen, flowers from the garden and conservatory were cut and taken into Margaret Beale's flower room for arranging and, according to Muthesius, even in a simple workman's cottage the kitchen table was covered with a cloth at meal times and decorated with a potted plant.[7] In houses where gardening was not a passion and servants were few, transforming the table into a work of art each day (conceived in part as a means of keeping idle hands busy), was regarded as onerous. In a chapter on wasted domestic labor, written in 1918, Clementina Black wrote of the "increased daintiness and variety in cookery and table service" and the greater delicacy of table decoration which had developed in her own lifetime. "I do not remember that in any house known to my childhood flowers were usually to be seen in living-rooms, nor ever—at any meal partaken of by the young—on dining-tables. To-day, in the houses of persons neither less busy nor more amply provided with servants I see flowers as a matter of course, and indeed, expect to see them in my own."[8] More cultivated and able servants were becoming essential, she complained, "at the very time when the better members of the class from which servants are recruited are turning away from the occupation."[9]

The master of the house presided over dinner but it was the mistress who gave the cook her instructions, often going through the menu with her at the table after breakfast, and she was ultimately responsible for the quality of the food and the finesse with which it was served. Large dinner parties where the food was intended to impress were relatively unusual in Britain. The formalities of the meal were maintained for the family on a daily basis, however, and in addition to the dinner associated with the weekly "At Home," visitors were often invited to stay to lunch or dinner quite spontaneously. *The House* published complete menus every month for a "recherché little dinner for six," with the dishes named in French, and for simpler "home dinners. . .all in plain English." Recipes from magazines were provided, and although the mistress of the house was not expected to enter the kitchen, she needed to tread a delicate path between coaxing the best service out of the cook and checking that the expenditure on ingredients and other supplies did not escalate to unmanageable levels.

The hierarchy that determined the seating arrangements around the table was mirrored in the positions of the staff, who stood in attendance at the sides of the room and served in silence. An experienced butler, assisted by a maid, would serve the soup, carve the meat, and pour the wine as well, but "one New York butler latterly refused to wash dishes, telling his mistress that it would ruin his finger nails."[10] He was excused on the grounds that his skills in the dining room made him a consummate servant, "who laid the table and attended it with an ease and grace that gave his mistress that pleasant feeling of certainty that all would go well."[11] It was essential that the butler and the serving maid should be healthy in appearance and scrupulously clean. In smaller houses, where there was no butler, the maid was often chosen for her poise in the dining room, and the conventions of her black dress with starched collar and cuffs, white apron, and cap with streaming ribbons were as strict as those of the laid table.

The proportions of the dining room were dependent upon the size and shape of the table. Usually rectangular in plan with a fireplace in one of the short sides of the room and a sideboard against the adjacent wall, the dining room was furnished, ideally, with two doors. The first of these, entered from the hall or living room, was for the family and guests; the second, a service door, connected with the butler's pantry and the kitchen beyond. In smaller houses where the family served themselves, a hatch was cut between the kitchen and the dining room and framed to resemble a cupboard, while the basement kitchen in many town houses was connected to the dining room by a small service elevator with a hatch. The positions of the doors in all of the rooms in the Arts and Crafts home were carefully planned to protect the privacy and comfort of the occupants. They were placed as far as possible from the main sitting area to avoid unnecessary drafts and they usually opened inward toward the corner of the room so that the complete interior was not revealed at once. This also gave those inside the room a second to compose themselves when they heard the door handle turn. In the dining room, the service door was close to the sideboard so that dishes could be carried in and out to the kitchen with ease.

Soup tureens and dishes of cooked vegetables were placed on the sideboard and from there were served to the table. It was customary at smaller family gatherings for a joint of meat or a complete fish to be placed on the table and carved by the master of the house, but at larger dinners the butler would carve the meat at the sideboard. At Standen, James Beale stood at the sideboard to carve the roast beef, attended by his butler from Holland Park (who was later dismissed for drunkenness). It was the butler's task to advise, in a hushed tone, on the appetites of each of the diners and his information on one occasion coincided disastrously with an awkward silence around the table. When Beale asked "Who next?" his reply that it was one of the ladies who enjoyed a substantial helping was audible throughout the room.[12] Drawers were built into the sideboard for essential utensils and for the table linen in houses where there was no butler's pantry; a cupboard was provided below for wine and other drinks which could be locked away "since many English servants are fond of the bottle."[13] The wine was poured by the butler from crystal decanters which were set at either end of the table and carafes of water were also provided. The port glasses were not set out until the end of the meal, when the hostess would indicate that it was time for the ladies to withdraw.

The heaviest, most highly polished elements of the Victorian dining room were undermined by the Arts and Crafts Movement, and decorative reforms coincided with a period of gradual changes in dining procedures. The massive mahogany tables, somber color schemes, and thick curtains and blinds blocking out the sunlight for most of the day—which led *The House* to reiterate the witticism "that of all melancholy functions

ABOVE: Claret pitcher by Christopher Dresser. Wines were decanted and bottles were never placed on the Arts and Crafts table. In conventional dining rooms the port was not brought out until the ladies had withdrawn to the drawing room.

short of a funeral, an English dinner is the most depressing"—were lightened and simplified. Muthesius observed that a new practice, "known as *diner à la russe*," whereby the food was put onto plates before it was brought to the table, was also breaking down ancient customs: "its justification is that it saves time and formalities."[14] He attributed the more refined and cheerful decoration of the room to feminine influences, noting that it was no longer the custom to remove the cloth after dinner so that men could settle down to a hearty evening's drinking.[15] The dining room doubled as a smoking room in smaller Arts and Crafts homes but at the end of the meal, when the women withdrew to take their coffee in the drawing room, the men were not always left to their brandy and cigars. As smoking was synonymous with assertive behavior among progressive women, issues of equality which were paraded on the streets with embroidered banners could be claimed in the dining room by the comparatively simple means of remaining seated after dinner and reaching for the cigarette case.[16]

In cold weather the dining room was one of the warmest rooms in the house. Central heating was in its infancy and, after the bedrooms, the open fire in the dining room was one of the first to be lit before breakfast. In many houses it was the only room to be kept warm throughout the day, replacing the drawing room as the main sitting area for the family in the winter; comfortable chairs were provided so that in smaller houses the family could retire to the fireside after dinner. "The warmth and comfort of the dining-room on a winter evening will often make an adjournment to the drawing-room undesired where the fire, perhaps, has not been lighted till late and a general chilliness prevails. The dining-room thus becomes a place not severely set apart for meals, but to some extent a living-room for the family."[17]

In the Arts and Crafts dining room the fireplace was often housed within an inglenook or recessed to create a cozy sitting area away from the table. The "soothing and draft-defying charms" of compact winged armchairs became fashionable but the importance of retaining and enhancing the dining room's traditional warmth was countered by a contradictory need to correct its darkness.[18] Although in the evening a soft light over the table was considered desirable, great claims were made for the physical and psychological benefits of natural light during the Arts and Crafts period. "We all know the value of sunlight as a health-giving agent to the physical system, and it is not less so to our moral and spiritual natures. We absorb light, and it nourishes us with strange power. We are more active under its influence, think better, and work more vigorously."[19] Designers were careful to distinguish between the quantity of natural light in the drawing room and the more subdued effect appropriate for the dining room,

but larger windows were provided, even at the risk of creating drafts, and the colors and materials in the dining room were lightened accordingly.

The Arts and Crafts dining room was designed to make the essentials of gracious living accessible to the aspiring middle classes and to eliminate the pomp from the weekend retreats of the more affluent. Of all the rooms in the house, though, it was the most resistant to stylish innovations: "An Englishman would suspect you of every other revolutionary tendency, if you proposed any radical changes in the color of the walls [of the dining room], or in the forms and arrangement of the furniture." The traditional components of the room were modified rather than eliminated, and the family silver and good antique and reproduction furniture often coexisted with Arts and Crafts decorative schemes.[20] The tradition of paneling the dining room with a dark stained wood

LEFT: "Peacock and Dragon" chair backs, designed by Morris, protected the diners at Standen from the roasting effects of the open fire.

RIGHT: The steel cheeks and smoke cowl to Philip Webb's dining-room fireplace at Standen were crafted by John Pearson to cast a pattern of reflections from the open fire into the room.

covered with layers of varnish—"something advertised and smelly," which one writer suggested was smeared on for amusement on rainy days—gave way, in more enlightened households, to plainer effects; and the use of richly figured woods such as walnut was superseded by lighter timber.[21] Modern methods of cutting timber by machine reduced the cost of paneling at the end of the nineteenth century, and architects such as Voysey designed plain batten-and-bead wainscoting in oak with built-in furniture to convey a cottage simplicity.[22] In houses where the budget precluded the cost of hardwood, pine (or "deal" as it was known then) was the next best thing but it was always painted.[23] No self-respecting joiner would suffer the knotty irregularities of exposed pine. Warm colors which suggested repose were chosen in place of the darker tones of the Victorian dining room.

Webb's paneling for the dining room at Standen is painted green, "a soothing background to the loaded table, with its candles, flowers and silver."[24] The color is complemented by the steel cheeks and smoke cowl of the fireplace, designed by Webb and crafted by John Pearson, with a steel plate rack and fender made by Thomas Elsley. The paneling is flush with the fireplace, as it is in the drawing room, but the proportions are bolder in keeping with the more masculine treatment of the room; one critic remarked that he could imagine ladies exclaiming, "Oh! I should not like anything like that!"[25]

Webb was, in fact, acutely aware of the preferences and requirements of his clients, and although the dining room at Standen defies Victorian conventions by facing south, the importance of introducing more light into the room was qualified by the position of the drawing-room bay, immediately to the west, which partially shades the windows in the afternoons. They are screened by holland blinds and woolen "Peacock and Dragon" curtains woven by Morris & Co. Webb wrote to Margaret Beale after a site visit in July 1894 that the sun had been burning hot until 4:30 in the afternoon, but the house had remained perfectly cool: "While having my dinner in the dining room (which should have been in the servants hall, but your butler insisted on trying to make a gentleman of me) I could not but enjoy looking through a partly open window on the south and seeing the lovely wooded hill on the other side of the valley: and this—perhaps—the more so, that I had to refrain from a lovely fruit pie, and strawberries with cream, set out to tempt me from the path of wisdom!"[26]

ABOVE: Muffin dish by C. R. Ashbee with more elaborate and conventional silver cake basket behind. Arts and Crafts designers delighted in simplifying the ordinary objects of everyday use.

RIGHT: The dresser was an item of kitchen furniture until it was elevated and refined by Arts and Crafts designers for the dining room. This example by Philip Webb is one of a pair designed for Standen. The red walnut table is eighteenth century.

William Nicholson's portraits of Margaret and James Beale were taken to Standen after their London house was sold in 1912 and hung, in accordance with tradition, in the dining room.[27] In more modest houses, where neither paneling nor portraits were appropriate, the artistic fabrics and wallpapers of the Arts and Crafts Movement provided a modern and economic alternative to the tapestry hangings and oil paintings in heavy gilt frames typical of Victorian dining rooms. Woven fabrics by Morris and later designers were treated as heirlooms and moved from one home to the next. They were hung from small brass rings stitched into the backing, which were looped through hooks or onto a slender brass rod just beneath the picture rail so that they could be easily removed for washing. When patterned papers were used there was an emphasis on harmonious designs and muted colors in order to aid digestion.

All of the family meals were taken in the dining room, and Standen was furnished by the Beales with a mahogany dining table and reproduction Queen Anne chairs that followed a contemporary fashion for mahogany furniture in a more delicate eighteenth-century style. Webb's proposal for a sideboard was not executed, but two dressers made to his designs were built into a deep east-facing bay which lights the room in the early morning. Breakfast was a substantial meal in the Arts and Crafts home; every member of the family was expected to appear punctually in the dining room, where cooked dishes were set out on a sideboard or dresser. Porridge and hot scones were customary at Standen. It was traditional for the mistress of the house to serve coffee from a silver urn and although the rituals at breakfast were more relaxed than at dinner, generally speaking, there were concerns in the Arts and Crafts period that domestic standards must not be allowed to slip too far. Breakfast in bed was encouraged only on rare occasions—on the morning after a ball, for example, or in cases of illness. In addition, a woman's dress and deportment at breakfast, according to *The Ladies' Home Journal*, were the key to a successful marriage: she should never allow her husband to see her less carefully or tastefully dressed than during the days of their honeymoon.[28] Reading letters at the table was frowned upon, and gentlemen were chastised for falling into the increasingly common habit of reading the newspaper at breakfast. "Putting aside even the main point, the disrespect which such a habit shows to the wife and those at the breakfast table, it practically robs one of the two meals which the average man eats in his home of all sociability and possibility of domestic talk."[29]

The importance of acquiring immaculate table manners, of sitting and speaking with perfect decorum as well as knowing which knives and forks to use meant that children were allowed down from the nursery for Sunday lunch as soon as they were old enough to meet the demands of the occasion. Linen covers were used to protect the embroidered chair seats when the older children were "promoted" to the dining room at Standen, but discipline was strict, and if they misbehaved James Beale would look over their heads to the wall as if they no longer had a presence in the room.[30]

In other houses the dining room was occasionally requisitioned in the afternoons as an informal space for family activities set apart from the refinement of the drawing room. Mary Lutyens took all her meals in the nursery and seldom saw her father as a consequence. She later recalled that, to entertain her after Sunday lunch, he would make drawings on the dining-room table ("made realistic with the help of mustard"). "One of these, a particular favourite, was called The Relief of Lady Smith and can no doubt be imagined."[31] Although they had the disadvantage of always being wiped away, the process of revealing the subject of the drawing, line by line, was part of a shared intimacy.

Lutyens's fantasies about married life during his 1897 engagement took the form of interior designs, sketched and described in letters to Lady Emily. He imagined the decoration of the table at breakfast with breads, fruit, and flowers and described the food, "crisp curling bacon in its casserole, on occasions of great state a sausage! hams and eggs. . .and tempting toast upon a bright iron grid before the fire."[32] He designed an oak refectory table and a double bed for their new house, and his drawings and descriptions of the table—with individual blue linen cloths, white china, green-handled cutlery, and a pair of brass candlesticks for each place setting—illustrate an emotional commitment to his impending marriage materialized in the design of everyday objects.[33]

His letters describe an architectural vision of the dining room in which every detail down to the "papery pot-pourri" (to be provided by Gertrude Jekyll), was considered and prescribed as a setting for family life. The "great sheet of superfine damask" was to be dispensed with so that the plain wood of the table should be seen "peering up" through spaces between the blue linen. He also described how afternoon tea, significantly, was to take place in the dining room rather than the drawing room (he did not offer to pour). Lady Emily was promised a white dining room but when the house in Bloomsbury Square was leased, the walls were painted red (color theorists of the day would have drawn conclusions), contrasting with a green painted floor and a few old rugs. The striking effect of the decor was almost equaled by the force with which the table framework connected with the knees of unsuspecting guests.[34] Lutyens's artistic vision, in spite of the romantic nature of his descriptions and his desire to please his future bride, was scandalously unconventional.

The introduction of bare oak, daringly revealed in the Arts and Crafts table, with only a few strips of linen, criss-crossed to indicate the place settings, was more shocking, initially, than the straight heavy legs, which usurped the curvaceous lines and carved details of more traditional dining tables and chairs.[35] In fact, the sight of a naked tabletop at mealtimes was regarded as "the quintessence of barbarity" in Victorian society. Morris was probably the first designer to abolish the cloth, and his habit of setting up a long oak table in the drawing room at Queen Square for special dinners demolished more than one rule of etiquette.[36]

Arts and Crafts furniture in both Britain and America had its origins in the experimental designs of artists and architects such as G. E. Street, Ford Madox Brown, and Rossetti, as well as Morris and Webb who sought out what they believed to be basic and uncorrupted forms of design in cottage furniture. This early Arts and Crafts furniture of the 1860s refuted the senseless ornament and superficial historicism of Victorian furniture styles. It was sometimes deliberately barbaric and crudely experimental, as in Morris's medieval-inspired designs for Red Lion Square, but the rush-seated chairs of Morris & Co.'s Sussex line were light and elegant enough to be compatible with more established furniture styles.

A younger generation of architects, including W. R. Lethaby, Ernest Gimson, and Sidney and Ernest Barnsley, developed the ethos of cottage furniture into a coherent Arts and Crafts style in the 1890s. They were all members of the Society for the Protection of Ancient Buildings and were profoundly influenced by Webb and Morris. One critic noted that the only part of the house never to have succumbed to the excesses of Victorian design was the kitchen and so deduced that the idea of the new movement in design, "very wholesome so far as it went, was to spread the kitchen over the rest of the house."[37] Plain wooden tables and dressers were exhibited at the Arts and Crafts Exhibitions in London "with every pretence of being works of art." Muthesius later claimed that the only difference between these new designs and real kitchen furniture was that they were ten times more expensive and that the public remained scornful of their merits, but they were generously reviewed in *The Studio* and other magazines.[38]

RIGHT: Detail of an oak dresser, designed by Sidney Barnsley for Rodmarton Manor.

The new furniture was perfectly compatible with the Arts and Crafts ideal of the simple life and it was uniquely suited to the modern middle-class cottage or bungalow, in which distinctions between separate rooms were in a state of creative flux. By making the kitchen table (a sturdy piece of furniture topped with heavy oak or deal planks for the preparation of food) a model for the dining room, and by adapting the dresser from a storage fixture for pots and pans to a more presentable form that could double as a sideboard, the Arts and Crafts Movement laid the groundwork for the combined kitchen and dining room as a family living space.

Most houses were managing with fewer servants, and many middle-class householders were content to serve themselves at breakfast and lunch, if not at dinner, which meant the fusion of kitchen utility with the culture of the dining room that the new furniture was designed to suggest catered to a timely reduction in ceremony. It presented its architect designers, nevertheless, with significant problems. The workmanship involved in making the pieces was often rudimentary and the art of simplicity was easily imitated. Shops and manufacturers sent their cribbers to Arts and Crafts exhibitions "to parody anything in which there seem[ed] to be a chance of money," and sketching from the pieces on display had to be prohibited.[39]

According to their detractors, most of the furniture at the Arts and Crafts exhibitions did not venture beyond the "ABC of carpentry": yawning miters, gaping joints, and cabinet drawers that would not open made the pose of craftsmanship a point of ridicule.[40] Designers such as Sidney Barnsley and Ernest Gimson sought to justify the artistic status and the relatively high cost of uniquely designed and crafted furniture by differentiating their pieces from ordinary workshop standards with complex joints and inlays which required a masterly skill in execution. Early in their careers they founded the firm of Kenton and Co. (in 1890), together with the architects Mervyn Macartney, Reginald Blomfield, and W. R. Lethaby, with the aim of developing good design in modern furniture. The firm was set up, taking Morris & Co. as a model, in a spirit of amateur enthusiasm but unlike Morris the partners kept their hands clean. Lethaby later recalled how they each put in £100 at the start to take a workshop and employ a foreman, who supervised the execution of their designs by professional cabinetmakers. "We enjoyed ourselves greatly for about two years, making many pieces of furniture, selling some at little over cost price—nothing being included for design or for the time expended by the proprietors."[41] The enterprise was not a commercial success and perhaps, given the partners' commitments as architects, it was not intended to be more than an exploratory expansion of their other work. However, Gimson moved to Gloucestershire with the brothers Ernest and Sidney Barnsley to set up a new furniture workshop (initially at Ewen and then at Sapperton near Cirencester) to create elaborately designed and crafted pieces with simple "cottage-style" work that could be built by trained village craftsmen in order to make the business socially and economically more viable.[42]

At this time, Gimson apprenticed himself (for how long is not known) to Philip Clissett who had been making rush-seated chairs with tall backs in a village near Ledbury since 1838. The preservation of traditional rural crafts and the communities they sustained was an area of concern among many Arts and Crafts designers, and the classic design and craftsmanship of Clissett's chairs had already been recognized by the Art Workers' Guild. The timber was cut from young ash and oak trees grown locally and the chairs were made while it was still green so that the joints shrank and held tight as the wood dried without the use of screws to hold them together. The chair backs and legs were turned on a simple pole-lathe and the curved back pieces were boiled in a copper before being left to dry in a bending frame. Rushes for the seats were bought from a man who gathered them from the banks of the Thames River each summer. In sum the chairs were made simply and cheaply using local materials in the traditional way.

Gimson used to joke that Clissett kept all his orders in a teapot on the kitchen mantel shelf. When he had a batch of chairs ready he would take an order out of the pot and send the chairs to that address; if the order was too large for the number available he would simply put it back and take another one out instead. He wondered whether those people with orders at the bottom of the pot ever got their chairs.[43] Gimson altered the proportions and some of the details of Clissett's design and his version of a tall ladder-back rocking chair was a best-seller at the 1893 Arts and Crafts Exhibition.[44] Its appeal was founded in part on its comparative cheapness, selling for only a pound, but a sympathy for the integrity and manual skill entailed in making each chair made it one of the staples of the Sapperton workshops, and its unassuming cottage style meant that it could be used as an occasional chair in the dining room or elsewhere in the house. When he became too busy to make the chairs himself Gimson trained one of the young men from the local sawmill, Edward Gardiner, to specialize in making them so that the skills were perpetuated; the chairs are still being made in the traditional way today.[45]

Although Morris had moved to Kelmscott Manor, less than twenty miles to the east of Sapperton, in 1871, Gimson and the Barnsleys were the first Arts and Crafts designers to

RIGHT: The attractions of country life were not taken too seriously in Hilda Benjamin's portraits of Rodmarton villages at work and play. Appliquéd by the Rodmarton Women's Guild in the 1920s, they demonstrated the enduring qualitites of Rodmarton's craft traditions.

establish their studios and workshops in the Cotswolds with the intention of working with local craftsmen and reviving vernacular traditions. Unlike Ashbee's much larger Guild of Handicraft, comprising about fifty men and their families who moved to Chipping Campden nine years later in 1902, Gimson and the Barnsleys became an integral part of the local community. They enlisted the support and involvement of the village wheelwright and blacksmiths so that the specialist skills of a largely agricultural community were absorbed into their designs. In addition, their commissions were crafted by local men, regenerating the village economy and instilling a new appreciation of good design and fine workmanship. Sidney Barnsley wrote to Webb of a hope that in time the workshops would form a nucleus around which others would attach themselves and the group were often visited by friends and colleagues as well as clients from London.

The architects Detmar Blow and Alfred Powell, who became better known in later years for his work as an artist potter, were frequent visitors. Dorothy Walker, a student at the Slade and the daughter of Morris's printer, Emery Walker, wrote in her diaries of impromptu picnics and games of croquet with Gimson, Powell, and the Barnsleys while her father was at Kelmscott in the summer of 1899. Detmar Blow arrived toward the end of her stay and she wrote with great excitement of a tea party hosted by the architect Robert Weir Schultz—"No Chaperones admitted. We had great fun. I poured"—but the following week she was whisked back to London with her father, taking books created by Morris's Kelmscott Press for loan to the Arts and Crafts Exhibition.[46]

The preservation of vernacular traditions became a guiding principle in every aspect of life and work for Gimson and the Barnsleys—from collecting berries for sloe gin each autumn to the styling and construction of buildings and their interiors. The workshops were sustained by enlightened patronage but in the commission to build and furnish Rodmarton Manor, a few miles south of Sapperton, they encountered a client whose extraordinary commitment to craftsmanship as a means of binding a village community together matched their own. The Honorable Claud Biddulph was a wealthy London banker; he and his wife, Margaret, initially engaged Ernest Barnsley to design them a country cottage at Rodmarton. As the medieval manor house to their estate had been demolished earlier in the nineteenth century, however, leaving the village without a focus, they were persuaded instead to commit an annual sum of £5,000 per year (at a time when £500 would build a small cottage) to build and furnish a new manor house, generating a steady source of employment for the rural community. "It seems that once work was underway, Ernest Barnsley elaborated the possibilities of the venture so beguilingly that his client's enthusiasm kindled and Rodmarton became not only a large country house but a centre for crafts and the education of the tenantry."[47] The building was constructed, decorated, and furnished without the aid of machinery, using timber felled from the estate and slate and stone quarried nearby. Local craftsmen, many of them learning their trades during the course of construction, provided the labor force, and the exceptionally long duration of the building work, which began in 1909 and continued until 1926 (with an interruption during the First World War), established standards of skill and commitment that Ashbee, when he visited the estate in 1914,

LEFT: Appliquéd curtains in the chapel at Rodmarton Manor.

ABOVE: The great hall at Rodmarton Manor, looking westward toward the drawing room.

believed to be unsurpassed. "I've seen no modern work equal to it. . .And when I ask why I find the answer in the system, the method rather than the man. It is a house built on the basis not of contract but of confidence."[48]

The principal rooms at Rodmarton face south, with an immense living hall sandwiched between the drawing and dining rooms. They were never occupied in a conventional manner by the Biddulphs because, having moved into the first part of the house to be completed, the service wing, they were reluctant to expand into the larger rooms, and the hall and drawing room became absorbed into the social and artistic experiment of the construction of the house. The hall was used for village theatricals and other entertainments rather than the extravagant balls that its dimensions suggest and Margaret Biddulph's elegant drawing room was photographed for *Country Life* in 1931, furnished with long trestle tables and benches as a workroom where village craftsmen and women practiced basketmaking, embroidery, and needlework. Curtains for the house were embroidered and appliquéd by the villagers and the modern tradition of

craftsmanship that Rodmarton encouraged inspired a series of hangings depicting village life—featuring portraits of particular individuals and their animals designed by Hilda Benjamin and executed by the Rodmarton Women's Guild.

Country Life reported that "a great deal of furniture-making goes on in the house." The Biddulphs combined solid, straightforward pieces constructed by the villagers with exhibition-standard work commissioned from Gimson and Sidney Barnsley or purchased as finished pieces from their workshops. Because the manor has remained in the Biddulph family, pieces have been added to the original furnishings over the last three generations. The firedogs in the dining room, for example, were designed by Gimson for his own house and crafted by the local blacksmith, Alfred Bucknell, who produced most of his metalwork. The brass wall sconces were designed by Norman Jewson who married Ernest Barnsley's daughter Mary, and there are dishes and an armorial vase by Alfred and Louise Powell. The dining room at Rodmarton was decorated and furnished with a cottage-style simplicity, scaled up to manorial proportions. The walls were whitewashed. There may have been an intention to panel them but the policy of drawing all the oak for the house from the estate meant that some rooms had to wait for their paneling until the trees were ready for felling and the timber had seasoned. There are very few mature oaks left on the estate today. The drawing room was not paneled until the 1930s. The light simplicity of the interior is an appropriate setting, however, for the plain oak tables and dresser designed by Sidney Barnsley which fuse the aesthetics of the modern kitchen and the medieval manor with a quality and style of workmanship that was both innovative and distinguished.

ABOVE: Firedogs designed by Gimson for his own house and crafted by Alfred Bucknell.

RIGHT: The Rodmarton Manor interiors and their furnishings are a testament to sustained patronage.

Barnsley paid homage to the strength and ingenuity of local woodworking traditions in the design of one of the tables for Rodmarton. The underframing was constructed using a combination of hayrake and wishbone joints, developed over several centuries by wheelwrights and other craftsmen for farm carts, wagons, and agricultural tools. In adapting them for the first time to furniture design, Barnsley enhanced the visual effect of solidity and durability of the table by chamfering the stretchers to accentuate the handworkmanship and surface texture of the oak table. As a skilled craftsman Sidney Barnsley was exceptional among architects of the Arts and Crafts Movement, most of whom left the execution of their furniture designs to cabinetmakers, and he deliberately embraced the challenges of working in oak. He described the physical demands of handling massive lengths of timber in a letter to Webb written in 1904 when he had just completed two oak tables each twelve feet in length.[49] The tabletop at Rodmarton is constructed from three planks joined with wedged double dovetails:

the joints cut through the thickness of the wood in a display of strength and dexterity which contradicts the appearance of effortless simplicity suggested by the austere lines of the design.

Unlike Gimson, who employed up to fifteen craftsmen in his workshop, Sidney Barnsley worked alone, executing all of his own work with the exception of one piece: the monumental oak dresser, designed for the dining room at Rodmarton, was built in the carpenter's shop by Claud Biddulph's estate workers under the supervision of his foreman, Alfred Wright, as if it were part of the interior joinery. The dresser was conveniently situated next to the service door in a recess in the north wall of the room to avoid obstructing the space around the tables. When *Country Life* visited the house in 1931 it was described as "typical of the clean, straight forward design and high quality of workmanship which characterise all the furniture of the Barnsley-Gimson school."[50]

The Arts and Crafts dresser and the conventional sideboard converged in form toward the end of the nineteenth century, and Barnsley's design is characteristic of pieces that combined the attributes of both types. Traditionally the sideboard had no useful upper part, comprising cupboards and drawers beneath a surface for serving food. The dresser, a much larger piece of furniture, was equipped with four or five substantial shelves running the full width of the piece above a base which was furnished with drawers and enclosed cupboards, or left open with a single deep shelf for large utensils. Late Victorian sideboards acquired glazed cupboards and shelves above the serving surface, but for Arts and Crafts designers, the kitchen dresser was a more attractive model for reform. The upper shelves to the Rodmarton dresser are flanked by narrow cupboards and backed by a framework of paneling, breaking up the massive proportions of the piece, and the cabinets beneath are discreetly decorated with a pattern of projecting panels.

The handcrafting of the building and its furnishings at Rodmarton was loaded with issues of social responsibility. The uncompromising clarity of Ernest Barnsley's architecture and his brother's furniture was symptomatic of the strength of their determination to establish a viable alternative to the values and consequences of industrialization. Dining-room furniture which was produced in batches, however, without the physical involvement of the designer, could also be charged with specific messages. Voysey's furniture designs were made up by a few favored cabinetmakers who could be depended upon to follow his instructions precisely and to produce work of a consistently high quality. Voysey was tolerant of machine methods of production, urging his fellow designers to accept that the days of cheap labor were over and that their wood would be delivered machine-sawn and machine-planed. He believed that it was the modern designer's duty to work within these constraints, avoiding the graceful curves to arms and legs which could only be worked by hand. However, he was equally convinced that the forms of his dining tables and chairs and the untreated white oak of which they were made could inspire their users with noble thoughts and feelings which would improve their characters as well as their behavior. The master and mistress of the house, he wrote, were to have high-back dining chairs with arms, while their family and friends

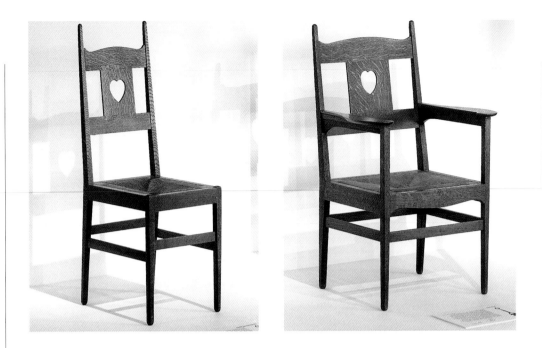

were to be given chairs with low backs and no arms. His reasons were partly practical: unless the chairs were spaced widely apart, high backs obstructed the servants' waiting at table. However, his preferences were founded on a more esoteric philosophy. The high backs and arms for the host and hostess, according to Voysey, were associated with kingship and self control, and the straight, upright proportions of his dining chairs encouraged a suitably erect and disciplined posture.[51]

Dining chairs were purchased in batches of six, eight, twelve, or twenty, and when they were not in everyday use they were lined up against the sides of the room. Voysey designed both leather and rush-seated chairs for the dining room, in accordance with conventions, but Muthesius judged that, in general, rush seats were only tolerable when they were covered with a loose cushion. He found the English custom of providing the host and hostess with the most comfortable seats at the table inhospitable but the rationale, as he understood it, was founded not in kingship but in an entrenched idea that the armchair was the appropriate seat for the chairman or head of the company.[52]

The philosophical ideals that imbued the work of craftsmen and designers of the Arts and Crafts Movement were not always understood by their clients and customers. Voysey, for example, believed that the abstract form of the circle stimulated the intellect. He might have waited to observe an improvement in one of his clients, Mrs. Van Gruisen, after designing a dining room for her house in Birkenhead which featured a circular table beneath a circular lamp, with a circular mirror on the wall and a circular dumbwaiter next to an immense semicircular window. When the interior was published in *The Studio* and the German *Dekorative Kunst*, however, its intellectual claims were not made public and it is probable that Mrs. Gruisen, too, remained in ignorance.[53]

Nevertheless the English Arts and Crafts custom of offering lectures and texts to accompany and explain design innovations and to set them within a wider social and

LEFT: The elegant lines and upright simplicity of C.F.A. Voysey's dining chair (left) and carver (right) were designed to improve his clients' characters as well as their postures.

RIGHT: The dining room at 37 Bidston Road, designed by C.F.A. Voysey, with a theme of circles.

political context—beginning with Morris and his circle and continuing through the essays and lectures of the Arts and Crafts Exhibition Society—generated an informed reception for new work. The high moral ground of designer hypotheses could also be adapted to commercial ends, however, and in the writings of Gustav Stickley a laudable design philosophy was perfectly phrased and focused to open up and expand a space in the market for Craftsman products.

The furniture and domestic objects which Stickley promoted were not all handcrafted. Nor were their makers responsible for every stage in the production of each piece so that issues of authorship and creative satisfaction could be unequivocally celebrated. Craftsman products were more expensive than those of their competitors but they were distinguished by good design, impeccable workmanship, and fine materials, and it was precisely these qualities which were accentuated in Stickley's articles for *The Craftsman*. He flattered his customers by describing strength as a national characteristic. He claimed to believe that they would understand how each piece was put together because the details of construction were clearly expressed and that they would recognize in the sturdy designs and durable materials a sound investment which could be handed down to their children and future generations. Stickley's oak furniture was designed to appeal to families whose Craftsman homes were too small to afford a separate kitchen and dining room, still less a butler's pantry, as well as to more affluent homeowners. The monumental simplicity of his dining tables, sideboards, and chairs were tailored to furnish uncluttered interiors in which "hospitality and good cheer" superseded the oppressive atmosphere of Victorian dining rooms. The styling and finish of his furniture, however, was determined by practical and economic constraints as well as the ideological considerations which appear in Craftsman propaganda.

Oak was celebrated as "a robust, manly sort of wood" with a strength and austerity that suggested permanence and stability.[54] It was the most durable of native hardwoods but it was also relatively cheap and abundantly available at the turn of the century. The toughness and weight of the wood made it difficult to work, however, and its texture made it unsuitable for elaborate curves—which exposed the open grain to splitting. Stickley's furniture, like that of Voysey, made a virtue of these qualities. The straight legs and unadorned surfaces, depending for their effect upon the grain of the wood and the structure of the piece, were uniquely suited to oak. Stickley suggested that the warmer color and markings of plain-sawn oak made it preferable for wainscoting, but for table-tops, where large expanses of wood were required to take hard wear without warping or marking, quarter-sawn oak was used so that the curved and "glassy" rays which give the oak its strength bound the structure of the wood together. Quarter-sawn oak is more wasteful than cutting plain-sawn planks along the length of the tree. The trunk must be

A CRAFTSMAN DINING ROOM, WITH BUILT-IN SIDEBOARD AND RECESSED WINDOW

ABOVE: *The Craftsman* recommended warm colors for the dining room with textiles stitched by the mistress of the house to pull the decorative theme of the room together.

cut into quarters before the planks are cut at a 45-degree angle to the radius, but this extravagance was moderated by fuming the timber to even out any color variations between the planks and to produce a darker, more mellow tone, which could then be waxed or finished with a thin coat of shellac varnish.

Stickley's designs for dining rooms followed the conventions of the English country house. A well-fitted swinging door barricaded all sounds and smells from the kitchen but the butler's pantry—where the table linen, glasses, plates, and cutlery were kept in built-in cupboards—was replaced by a china cupboard built into the wall between the dining room and the kitchen. The sideboard, too, was built-in wherever possible and in south-facing dining rooms, where the glare of the sun would make meal times uncomfortable, it was positioned beneath an art glass window so that the room was suffused with colored light. In Stickley's drawings and watercolors for *The Craftsman*, the focus of the dining room was always the table, positioned in the center of the room beneath a low pendant lamp. The sturdy oak furniture, with rush- or leather-seated chairs drawn around the table, has an almost human presence, but instead of presenting the splendors of the meal, Stickley's perspectives are taken at more informal moments.

The table is laid for lunch, perhaps, or set with a single plate and glass, so that it is the decor rather than the dinner that attracts attention. Stickley recommended a "richness and decision" in the decoration of the dining room, using warm but plain colors where the walls were not paneled which, he wrote, would grow wearisome in a room that was lived in all the time. Where the living and dining rooms were arranged as a single L-shaped space the color scheme for the dining room was to tone with that of the larger space, "but even then it may strike a stronger and more vivid note in the walls, while the woodwork remains uniform throughout."[55] The practical components of the room all contribute to an effect of decorative vitality: the sideboard with art metal hinges and handles and a few well-chosen pieces of glazed earthenware arranged on its surface; the candlesticks and fruit bowl on the table; and the textiles from the plain-colored rug with a patterned border to the curtains and table linen.

The Craftsman dining room was designed as a totality but the preeminence of the laid table was dissipated. The impeccable starched white cloth was deemed inappropriate to the Craftsman home. In its place the coarser, more organic texture of homespun linen, unbleached or colored in natural tones from ivory to "warm pale brown" were recommended for table "scarves," which were appliquéd or embroidered with bold motifs drawn from nature where they hung over the table edge. Any woman, Stickley claimed, should be able to make her home interesting and beautiful by stitching "a snap of solid colour" into the table linen and curtains. By running the colors and patterns from the stenciled decoration of the walls through the curtains and carpets to the tablecloth, however, the Craftsman dining room undermined the fundamental strategy of ensuring that the meal and the rituals of its presentation should dominate the room. By presenting the dining room as an extension of the living space, the taut discipline of the room as the seat of patriarchal authority and the center of domestic control was effectively decorated away.

CHAPTER SIX

BEYOND THE GREEN BAIZE DOOR

LEFT: Dresser designed by W. R. Lethaby, built into the kitchen at Melsetter House.

"N THE WELL-REGULATED HOUSEHOLD, which is the ambition of all house-wives, the smooth running of the domestic machinery must depend on the efficiency of those offices, which, hidden away behind the baize-covered doors of the service passage, are not visible to the eyes of the visitor."[1]

The size of the service wing in the Arts and Crafts home depended upon the scale of the house, and the number of servants employed was directly related to the income of the household. It ranged from a labyrinth of corridors and separate rooms designed to serve the intricate needs of the larger country house to a single room, the kitchen, in the cottage or bungalow where no servants were employed or the staff was limited to a cook and a housemaid. Good servants were particular about their surroundings and, despite the socialist leanings of many Arts and Crafts designers, the quality of service that their clients hoped to enjoy was absolutely dependent upon providing the staff with modern and efficient working conditions and comfortable spaces in which to relax. A disgruntled cook was capable of waking the entire household at the crack of dawn in the course of bashing the range into submission to heat the water for morning baths. Clients who were enamored with the ideal of the simple life found that its charms were more achievable if the servants could be persuaded to harmonize with their surroundings.

ABOVE: The chapel in the west wing at Rodmarton Manor, designed by Ernest Barnsley.

Relations between servants and their employers changed significantly during the nineteenth century and the character of the Arts and Crafts service wing, including the provision of well-proportioned rooms, decorated with a degree of style and thoughtfully arranged to enjoy a favorable aspect and an attractive view, reflected a new regime based on mutual respect. The mistress of the house was responsible for every element of household management, no matter how large or small her staff, and at the beginning of the nineteenth century her authority had been absolute. She provided her servants with food, accommodation, and clothing, and she was entitled to tell them what to wear and how to behave in their leisure time as well as during the long hours of the working day. By the turn of the century, however, when there were plenty of alternative sources of employment, the balance of power had shifted. The role of the employer as guardian and protector, who was responsible for the moral improvement of the servants as well as their physical well-being, continued in rural communities. In country houses such as

Melsetter and Rodmarton Manor, chapels were provided so that the family and their servants could worship together every day. While sympathetic guidance was encouraged, however, servants in general claimed the right, "not always very judiciously or politely," to be treated as employees rather than dependents.[2]

Modern servants commanded competitive wages and the responsible employer abandoned the custom of perquisites, a form of gratuities where the housekeeper or cook took a percentage of the household bills from each tradesman, the old newspapers and wax candle-ends from the drawing room became the property of the butler, cast-off clothes were donated to the lady's maid, and, at the bottom of the chain, the scullery maid made a prize of the leftover cooking bones. A determination among servants to be free from "uncalled-for interferences" outside working hours meant that the same privacy which designers had always taken pains to secure for their clients, ensuring that the garden, for example, was never overlooked by the kitchen window, was extended to the service wing.

Beyond all the practicalities of designing efficient and attractive domestic quarters, however, the Arts and Crafts home was distinguished from its Victorian predecessors by a change in attitude toward servants. Victorian estate cottages for estate workers by architects such as George Devey had been picturesque because it had been fashionable to show a benevolent concern for the rural poor. In the Arts and Crafts home, the service accommodation was designed with the same rigor and integrity as the family wing. The dovecotes and cobbled enclosures of kitchen courts served as comfortable and convenient work spaces in which the rights of servants to respect and consideration were duly observed.

However, the mistress of the house retained overall control over the management of her home, and it was her prerogative to say exactly how and when each task should be

RIGHT: Behind the picturesque idealism of the kitchen court at Rodmarton, as at many Arts and Crafts houses, the work spaces of kitchen, scullery, pantries, and stores were well planned and furnished for the comfort and convenience of the servants.

ABOVE: The built-in oak furniture for the servants'
bedrooms at The Homestead, designed by
C.F.A. Voysey, was indistinguishable from that
of the guest bedrooms.

done. From childhood, women were trained by their mothers in housewifery and they were sternly warned that any ignorance of household duties would be exploited by disreputable servants and would ultimately lead to domestic conflict. "An untidy, ill-kept home, to say nothing of ill-cooked meals, is not conducive to the good temper or cheerfulness of a husband, more especially when he comes home after a hard day's work to find chaos reigning supreme."[3] While constant vigilance and strict discipline were a prerequisite of good management, however, kindness and sympathetic understanding were recommended as the most effective means of persuading servants to do their best work. The mistress who treated her servants with consideration—showing appreciation when good work was done and taking care that their health and safety was not jeopardized by running errands after dark, by standing outside on the sills to clean the windows, or by scrubbing floors without a soft mat on which to kneel (with the dreaded consequence of Housemaid's Knee)—would be rewarded, according to the household manuals of the day, by devoted and reliable staff. "Such a mistress would take care that her maids slept in well-ventilated, healthy rooms; that they had a sufficiency of covering on their beds in winter-time; that they had the means of taking baths when necessary, and of paying due regard to cleanliness."[4] Honorable and capable servants, it was argued, were produced in response to the same qualities in their mistresses.

The management of the Arts and Crafts home was standardized, in keeping with the immutable patterns of family life, and servants expected a degree of uniformity, not only in their daily tasks but also in the organization and equipment of the rooms in which they were to work. The relative comfort and convenience of the domestic quarters of different houses was known and discussed among servants who traveled with their employers when they visited friends for the afternoon or the weekend, but all servants were not equal in the eyes of their employers. Kitchen and parlormaids were relatively easy to replace and their training generally fell to the cook or the housekeeper. The process of finding a good cook, by comparison, was described as an agony and the responsible housewife was advised to have her kitchen "as well appointed in its own way as the drawing room, for the comfort of herself and of the household in general depends largely upon it, and she cannot expect to obtain and keep respectable servants unless she provides them with proper accommodation."[5]

In the larger Arts and Crafts home a butler and a housekeeper represented the master and mistress of the house respectively at the head of a small army of footmen and maids. The business of running the house was delegated with military precision and, in houses of a similar social status, the tasks and the timetable allotted to each member of the staff were remarkably similar. The Arts and Crafts designer needed to know the intricacies of every chore and its relation to the whole because the service wing was divided into a hierarchy of separate spaces, each designated to a particular servant's work. The butler's pantry was positioned to reflect his importance as the most educated and senior member of staff, but it was also designed and furnished to facilitate his practical responsibilities. Historically the butler's duties revolved around his expertise in caring for the household's wines and spirits; in fact, his title derived from that of "botteler" or "keeper of bottles." Wine was bought in the wood, and it was the butler's duty to bottle, cork, and seal it and to see to the conditions of its storage. He held the key to the cellar, kept stock of its contents, and decanted wines and other liquors when they were needed. In the majority of Arts and Crafts homes, however, his knowledge of fine wines and their storage was less important than his ability to serve the family and their guests and to deal effectively with all of the male members of staff, for whom he was responsible.

At the beginning of each day the butler ensured that all the fires were properly cleaned out and lit as appropriate. He brought in the breakfast and waited at the table, assisted by a footman in larger houses, and he delivered any letters and cards to his mistress on a silver tray. In smaller houses he went to the market and paid the bills, but the design of the butler's pantry and its position between the dining room and the kitchen were conditioned by his most prominent duties, answering the front door to visitors and attending to the arrangements for dinner. The butler's pantry was at the front of the house with a window overlooking the entrance so that approaching visitors would be seen in advance; the walls were lined with cupboards for glasses and china. He was responsible for setting the table, and the family silver as well as the finest tableware came under his supervision. The butler decided, in consultation with his mistress, what silver and glasses should be used for each occasion, and a sink was provided under the pantry window so that expensive china need not be entrusted to the attentions of the scullery maid. It was lined with lead, "against which china is less liable to chip or break than against any other substance," and the nozzle to the faucet was generally softened by a length of rubber tube.[6]

The silver was washed with hot soapy water and regularly cleaned with whiting, then polished with a fine dry chamois. Many butlers mixed their own polishing pastes and there were recipes to deal with different stains. Salt was rubbed into stains caused by vinegar and egg, and the persistent smell of food such as herrings on silver fish forks was dealt with by standing them in a basin of tea-leaves for a few minutes directly after washing. Silverware used only for special occasions was wrapped in soft tissue paper and then in a strip of green baize to prevent tarnishing and everyday silver cutlery was stored in a baize-lined drawer. The plate (gold or silverware) was always locked away at night and the butler's bedroom and the plate room at Melsetter, both opening off the butler's pantry, were typical of a compact suite of rooms at the operational heart of the house, with service stairs down to the basement kitchen and up to the bedrooms on the first floor.

As the last outpost in the journey from the kitchen to the dining room, the butler's pantry was inevitably used as a servery, and there was a counter above the lower cupboards or a table where dishes and utensils could be set down briefly during a large or elaborate meal. In American houses such as the Glessner House and the Gamble House, the butler's pantry was the only space between the kitchen and the dining room so that it was an essential thoroughfare at mealtimes. Americans regarded the English custom of maximizing the distance between the kitchen and the dining room (often running to dinner routes of more than a hundred feet in length) as excessive. The butler's pantry was fitted out as a simple work space, but the relative refinement of glazed cupboards displaying the best tableware, together with the immaculate tidiness of the room after the hectic conditions of the kitchen, established an important psychological as well as a physical transition from the service quarters to the family space. It acted as a barrier to any traces of undisciplined behavior, as well as to the sounds and smells of cooking in the kitchen.

In addition to his duties in the dining room, the butler was discreetly available in the billiard room and in the smoking room of larger houses when the gentlemen retired after dinner. The lamps and candles were in his care and at the end of the day, when the last drinks had been served and the family had retired to bed, his final task was to secure all the outer doors and windows and to be sure that the family was protected from every risk of theft and fire.

In wealthy families where the mistress was preoccupied with social engagements and in the homes of bachelors and widowers, the domestic responsibilities which a middle-class housewife would take on were delegated to a housekeeper. Described as "the brain of the establishment, while the domestics are the hands," her domain comprised a comfortably furnished room close to the butler's pantry where all the household expenses were accounted for.[7] The housekeeper was responsible only to the mistress of the house or to the master if he was unmarried. Like the butler, she served as an intermediary between the family and their servants and the management of the house was in her care. She provided for the needs of visitors, although her mistress decided which guests should be given adjoining bedrooms and whether their communicating doors were to be locked or left with the keys in place. She decided when and how the house should be cleaned, and the hiring and firing of maids was her responsibility. In a well-managed home the housekeeper and the cook enjoyed a relationship of mutual respect: "Nothing is more calculated to cause disturbance throughout the household than want of accord between herself and the cook."[8] The housekeeper ordered the meals and she was expected to understand cookery and even to prepare certain dishes herself, working in harmony with the kitchen staff. Theoretically she was required to supervise all their work but the authority of a skillful cook in the kitchen was governed with an element of deference.

In a large house the butler managed the male servants while the housekeeper organized the women and allocated their work. She rose early, at 6 or 6:30 A.M., as an example to the maids. "If the housekeeper is not about in the early morning, the work will be done in slipshod fashion, and everything will go wrong."[9] The cleaning and polishing of every inch of the interiors and the provision of clean linen and hot water for washing were among "the thousand-and-one details which come within her sphere." The best housekeepers, it was claimed, had spent a lifetime in service—gradually rising in rank from the most menial position so that they understood the daily routines of each of their subordinates.[10] In addition to the practical aspects of household management, the housekeeper was expected to keep a register of daily and weekly expenses, to check every bill and receipt, and to pay the other servants their wages. She kept an inventory of all the household articles—the ornaments, china, and bed and table linen which were in her charge—so that losses or breakages could be traced. She also decided when the furniture was to be renovated and the household linen replaced.

It was customary for a bride to bring a stock of linen as her contribution to the furnishing of the house. This supply was kept "in good order and spotless purity" in a built-in cupboard or a simple piece of furniture fitted with drawers and wide shelves that were strong enough to hold blankets, counterpanes, sheets, and tablecloths.[11] Embroidered monograms distinguished the plain white sheets and tablecloths for family use from those for the servants' quarters and if each bedroom was allocated its own separate linen, then the lettering was picked out in different colors. No scrap of linen was ever thrown away. Worn tablecloths were cut down for everyday napkins and tray-cloths; chamber pots were covered with the remnants of old towels and calico sheets; and chintz curtains were chopped up for dusters. When the daily usefulness of a cloth was completely exhausted, it was folded and stored in a "hospital drawer" to end its life as a dressing in a domestic emergency.

The housekeeper's room was close to the kitchen, and she held the keys to storerooms or cupboards for spices, biscuits, bottled fruit and sauces, and other valuable groceries. In country houses, remote from the nearest town or station, large reserves of food were necessary in case the roads were closed by bad weather or "a sudden influx of hungry guests should happen to arrive at dinnertime."[12] The housekeeper had her own small kitchen, known as a "still room" because historically the distilling of scents, essences, and liqueurs had been part of the art of housewifery. In summer fresh fruit from the gardens and orchards were bottled in the still room; it also could be used for preparing tea, coffee, and fancy cakes, but if the housekeeper's skills were questionable, she was advised "to leave cookery to the cook."[13] Most of the servants ate their meals and relaxed in the servants' hall. The upper servants took breakfast, tea, and supper in the privacy of the housekeeper's room, however, and dinner was served to them, either in that room or in the servants' hall, by one of the kitchen maids.

In affluent households a gentleman's valet and a lady's maid completed the contingent of upper servants. They attended to the personal needs of their employers, taking care of their wardrobes and the particulars of their appearances. A lady's maid needed to be skilled in hairdressing as well as dressmaking and millinery. She advised her mistress in matters of fashion, remodeling hats and bonnets with new trimmings or old ones salvaged from "cast-off head-gear," and she was responsible for altering and repairing dresses and for making up inexpensive materials "in an elegant and tasty fashion."[14]

RIGHT: Linen chest in the bedroom corridor at Rodmarton, designed by Peter Waals.

LEFT: Tennis and other sports were essential to the health and vigor of an Arts and Crafts lifestyle. In houses such as Rodmarton Manor which were too small for a gun room, designer cabinets kept rackets standing to attention ready for use.

In larger Arts and Crafts homes a sewing room was provided for her use with a constant northern light, but the duties of the lady's maid revolved around her mistress' bedroom and dressing room. She made the bed before dusting and tidying these rooms, and she laid out the clothing to be worn for each of the day's activities. The cleaning and storage of her mistress' garments was her responsibility, and she was required to sit up late in order to help her undress after social events and parties. She traveled with her mistress, taking charge of all the details of packing for a country-house weekend or a period abroad. Throughout the journey she attended to all her employer's needs while keeping an eye on the luggage and, when they arrived at their destination, she unpacked the trunks and helped her mistress dress before taking her place under the regime of an often unfamiliar housekeeper.

The importance of shooting, fishing, and other outdoor pursuits to country life necessitated a gun room close to the front door, stocked with equipment for every conceivable sport, and a drying room for wet clothes after the event. Although the valet and the lady's maid could delegate the most mundane tasks in the laundering and maintenance of their employers' clothes, they were held responsible for dealing decisively with damp and dirty garments. A warren of specialized rooms and stores was attached to the Arts and Crafts service wing so that the house was kept clear of wet raincoats and muddy boots. Because damp causes mildew and it was believed that wet furs were certain to attract moths, outdoor clothes were shaken or wiped with a soft cloth before being spread out to dry in the drying room. Clothes which were dried too quickly in front of a fire were prone to go stiff and even the expert attention of a skilled valet could not prevent expensive new clothes from turning limp and shabby when they were exposed to rain and fog. If coats were hung together on the same peg, depriving them of air, the "freshness" would be lost from the garments, so great care was taken to dry the clothes on racks. Wet trousers were pulled lengthwise and put in a press as soon as they were dry, and ladies were advised to keep about their person a strong piece of elastic with buttons at the front to fasten around their waists in case of a shower: "The back and sides of the dress can be lightly tucked into it in an instant, and thus the bottom of the dress will be effectually lifted out of the mud." [15]

Dry clothes were brushed in a brushing room to remove mud spots and dust before they were put away, and velvets and silks were wiped with a flannel cloth. A boot store was provided for wellingtons, and wet boots and shoes were stuffed full of paper by the valet or footman to prevent them from becoming hard and tight. Oil or grease was rubbed into their seams and creases to preserve them and, to keep them watertight, they were dressed with "dubbing" or good oil blacking. The soles of creaking boots were cured by oiling after a soak in salt and water, and leather shoes were "seasoned" for a few months before they were worn. In large Victorian country houses the boot store, the brushing room, the room for cleaning lamps and sharpening knives, stores for wood, coal, and refuse, and the coach house and stables were strung out in long wings. The most disciplined households insisted that workrooms for footmen and grooms were separated from their feminine counterparts: the bakehouse, the laundry, and the dairy were on opposite sides of the house. As smaller country houses became fashionable in the Arts and Crafts period, administered without a legion of footmen and maids, this lavish provision of specialized facilities was compressed. The gun room became a cupboard, for example, but the allocation of separate spaces for a hierarchy of chores remained in reduced form, even in the smallest service accommodation.

Although the position of the service wing was always secondary to that of the family accommodation, its orientation and outlook were carefully considered. It was usually arranged on the north side of the house around a courtyard or in a single wing that framed and sheltered the garden, and the windows looked out onto the street or the entrance court. It was considered improper for servants to linger in front of a window overlooking the family at their leisure and, where the conditions of the site made this unavoidable, designers resorted to tall hedges or walls to screen the garden from the kitchen and its yard. In order to light the bedroom corridor to the service wing of The Homestead in Frinton-on-Sea in Essex, Voysey set the windows above eye level and close to the ground so that the servants would have had to kneel to watch their employer

playing croquet. Their bedrooms and work spaces were generously lit, however, with north-facing windows looking out onto the street. The house was designed for a corner plot on a sloping site, and the narrow service wing, only one room deep, formed an L-shaped plan which wrapped round a large secluded rear garden. At the juncture of the two wings, Voysey made a clear visual distinction in the front elevation between the principal rooms and the domestic quarters. Above the dining room and the front door a striking composition of asymmetrical gables breaks the roof line. In contrast, the eaves to the adjoining domestic wing are brought down low to suggest a cottage simplicity so that the servants' bedroom windows are semidormers and the butler's pantry, the kitchen, and the scullery literally step down the hill in order of rank.

Voysey was not a socialist, and his houses in general conform to the convention that, where oak paneling was used in the family rooms, deal, painted cream or green, was good enough for the service wing. At The Homestead, however, he was able to persuade his bachelor client of the immorality of "building the back parts shabby."[16] He argued that architects and their clients should set an example to tradesmen by insisting that every part of the house, even the hidden places, be consistent in quality. In addition to the architectural creed of fitness for purpose—"It would not be consistent with fitness to use deal in my kitchen that I might have oak in my hall; it might be regarded by some as mere vulgar display"—he suggested that order and neatness in architecture were conducive to faithfulness and sincerity in the characters of the occupants of a house.[17] "If the money at our disposal will not pay for oak joinery everywhere, then let us have it nowhere."[18] At The Homestead the butler's pantry is lined with oak cupboards and the

LEFT: The bedroom corridor to the service wing at The Homestead was wainscoted in oak but deliberately designed with a window at knee height.

RIGHT: The entrance to The Homestead with the low eaves line and gables to the right marking the service wing.

kitchen is furnished with an oak dresser and built-in cupboards. Voysey was concerned with the happiness of his clients' servants as well as their integrity. Their rooms were well proportioned and in larger houses the servants' hall was distanced from the family wing so that both parties could be "reasonably merry" in private. "The laughing and talking in which one does not participate is not always pleasant."[19]

Very few Arts and Crafts kitchens have survived without modernization and those which have been preserved are in house museums. The kitchen was the most important room in the service wing. It was described as the working heart of the Arts and Crafts home and, whether it was in the basement, at the center of an extensive wing, or tacked onto the back of a bungalow, its organization and equipment required meticulous consideration.[20] No cleaning or washing up was permitted in the English kitchen. A separate scullery was attached even to the smallest cottage with a porcelain or earthenware sink for preparing meat, fish, and vegetables and for washing dishes. In smaller houses the scullery also served as a washroom equipped with large copper pots for boiling laundry. A wooden rack for draining plates was hung on the wall above the sink and, in larger houses where the scullery served as an overflow kitchen, the different washing chores were allocated to several kitchen maids at a row of specially designed troughs and sinks under the window. The dirtiest cleaning jobs were done outside, and the scullery was furnished with an exterior door but its connection with the working areas of the kitchen and the dining room beyond was more deliberately planned, so that the passage of food for the stove and dirty dishes from the table did not obstruct the flow of work. In Britain, the cook went into the scullery every time she needed to wash her hands, but sinks were admissible in American kitchens; the Arts and Crafts Movement introduced a move in Britain toward the "North Country practice" of dispensing with the scullery and building a sink close to the range in the "living and working kitchen" of the smaller home.

The cook was one of the most indispensable and highly valued members of the household and the kitchen was often designed to her specification. Mary Gamble's workbook, which lists the furniture and fittings for most of the rooms in the Gamble House, is left blank for the kitchen because its contents were not her concern. The cook's individual preferences were taken seriously, however, and in some cases the architect measured the height of the cook before he drew up the dimensions for the kitchen table.[21] The room was decorated as a functional work space with a high ceiling where the heat and fumes from cooking could gather and in large kitchens the ceiling was vaulted so that condensation would run down the walls instead of dripping. White tiles were used to accentuate the cleanliness of the space and the angles between the walls and floors were often curved to avoid dirty corners. Slate or stone slabs and tiled floors prevailed in old-fashioned kitchens but boarded floors were less conducive to rising damp and they were recommended because their spring made them more comfortable to work on. In really modern kitchens linoleum was laid as a cheap and easily maintained alternative to the daily scrubbing of traditional floors.

Opinions were divided over the best aspect for the kitchen. A south-facing room would have become an inferno from the heat of the range and a cool, north light was

LEFT: At Melsetter House vegetables from the garden were washed at an outdoor sink before they entered the scullery.

ABOVE: The Homestead kitchen was planned for the cook's convenience. The original range occupied the central, flat-arched recess so that the cook's work was lit from the left by a cool northerly light. The south-facing window on the right was originally screened by a pergola.

preferred, with the range recessed into the east wall so that the cook's work at the stove was always lit from the left. The case was made, however, that "this northern aspect for the kitchen constitutes real cruelty to cooks and deserves the attention of the Humanitarian League."[22] A thoughtful architect, it was argued, would not condemn the kitchen staff to labor all day without a ray of sunshine; a small east window was recommended as a supplement to the large north light for cross ventilation and "to give the day's work a cheerful start."[23]

In smaller houses where only a cook and a housemaid were employed, the cook's daily work started at 6:00 A.M. in summer and half an hour later in winter, when the kitchen fire was lit and the range cleaned and polished. In a large household the preparation of meals and the organization of well-stocked pantries and larders were the cook's sole responsibilities; she delegated the rough work of the kitchen to a number of maids. In more modest establishments, however, she swept and dusted the hall and dining room and, in the absence of any male servants, she was responsible for lighting the kitchen and dining-room fires and keeping the scuttles filled with coal. Breakfast was prepared for 9:00 A.M. and considerate employers did not expect porridge and omelets or dishes of grilled fish and kidneys unless they were prepared to pay a boy to sharpen the kitchen knives, to clean the master's boots, and to help with some of the heavy work. The cook cleared away the breakfast dishes and washed them up in the scullery. The "first coat" of grease was wiped away with old newspapers which were kept on a nail and burned after use to save the kitchen cloths and the dishes were then washed in hot water with soda and rinsed with cold water. Copper saucepans were cleaned with a mixture of salt and silver sand and stains were removed with a slice of lemon but by the turn of the century, aluminum pans were becoming increasingly popular: "Nothing is more easily kept clean than aluminium."[24]

The food was prepared at a sturdy kitchen table in the middle of the room which was generally designed by the architect or made to order. The tabletop of oak or deal planks was scrubbed with fine sand once or twice a week to keep it clean and white and a drawer was often provided at one end for the kitchen tablecloth "and other necessaries."[25] A wooden chair was provided for each servant and there were extra seats for their visitors because in smaller houses the kitchen doubled as the servants' hall but the remainder of the furniture was built-in. A large circular wall clock was often provided so that meals could be served within seconds of the appointed hour: "Punctuality is a virtue important to all, but indispensable in a cook."[26] Crockery for every day was stored on the open shelves of a large dresser and the pans and other utensils hung from a row of hooks screwed to the front of each shelf unless they were stowed away in the cupboards or on the pot-board below. Smaller utensils were kept in the dresser drawers but architects were advised that intricate and specialized storage fittings were wasted on the cook. "As a race they are prone to untidiness in their work, with a grand clear up at its conclusion, and much time and money is often expended in providing separate little compartments for each thing, with a result that they are never used for such purpose at all."[27] For the majority of cooks the necessity of turning out the kitchen to make "all clean for Sunday" meant that each separate compartment was another item to scrub.

All the crockery from the dresser shelves was taken down and washed every week and the shelves, cupboards, and drawers were scrubbed or wiped clean once a fortnight (painted cupboards were never scrubbed). Bright metal saucepans, dish covers, teapots, and coffeepots were scoured and polished, and the fur was removed from teakettles and boilers. The range was black-leaded, the flues were cleaned, the windows were washed, and the mats and rugs were taken outside to be brushed and beaten every week. In smaller houses the cook was also charged with cleaning the dining room, the hall, and the steps to the front door, but priority was given to the cleanliness of the cook's pantry and the larders where food was stored. The cook was entitled to one day off each month and once a week, usually on a Sunday, she was permitted to go out in the evening provided that the kitchen was tidy.

Refrigeration was a luxury in the Arts and Crafts home. Country estates occasionally invested in large refrigerating machines to make ice and to store game from a shoot until it could be used, but the compact kitchen fridge was only in its infancy.[28] Food was stored in pantries and larders away from the heat of the kitchen, and the flavor as well as the freshness of provisions were dependent upon the temperature and humidity of these storerooms or cupboards. "Much of the succulence and flavour of butcher's meat depends upon the length of time it is hung, but if it is kept in a moist close, or warm atmosphere, its flavour does not mature, and it speedily becomes putrescent."[29] Dairy products were kept in a cook's pantry and a separate meat larder was furnished with marble or slate shelves and fitted with rods and hooks for hanging meat. The pantry and larder were arranged on the north side of the service wing, within a convenient distance of the cooking range, and at least one exterior wall was fitted with a window of wire mesh. A similar panel in the opposite wall or door kept the store cool and well ventilated. In large country houses additional larders were kept for game and for fish, but they were located as far as possible from the living quarters "on account of their ineradicable smell."[30] On very hot days pails of water were left in the middle of the larders and flowerpots covered with wet cloths were set in soup plates filled with cold water to keep the temperature down. Their contents were protected from flies by metal meat covers and by wire frames covered with muslin. An ice chest or small refrigerated cupboard was kept in the cook's pantry for butter and milk.

Modern electrical appliances were regarded with suspicion in the home and although the technology was available to revolutionize the Arts and Crafts kitchen, servants

ABOVE: There were no built-in work surfaces,
in the Arts and Crafts kitchen. Food was
prepared at a central table and pots, pans,
and other cooking utensils were stored in a
built-in dresser.

whose employment depended upon labor-intensive methods and the maintenance of
familiar, if antiquated, equipment were resistant to change. "To the uninitiated there is
something mysterious in the force which cannot be seen; which, according to hearsay,
gives nasty shocks without provocation; and which in some uncanny way 'lights up hair
pins in little globes.'"[31] Conservative cooks were prone to hand in their notice rather
than accept an electric oven or even a kettle into the kitchen; "it is commonly
understood that every electric appliance is liable to explode."[32]

Old-fashioned arguments, however, were brought into play in the late 1890s to
promote the use of electricity in the kitchen. Cast-iron ovens, enameled inside and
heated by electricity, were cleaner and more efficient than the traditional range or gas
stove: "With electric cooking apparatus there is absolutely no smell and no dirt. . .the
quality and flavour of the meat or other food is better preserved," and because the
heat was generated by turning a switch and could be controlled at a constant

temperature, there was less chance of burning dinner.[33] Housewives were advised that their kitchens would need whitewashing less frequently, the servants would be less inclined to catch cold from working in overheated conditions, and the cleanliness and control of electricity would reduce the numbers of crickets and black-beetles in the service wing.

The manufacturers of electric cooking appliances separated the processes of grilling, boiling, frying, and roasting. They produced compact, free-standing electric hot plates, independent grills, and copper saucepans and stew-pans, as well as electric kettles and ovens which were recommended for their versatility: "Four chops can be grilled. . .and a kettle or other vessel boiled simultaneously." Electric irons obviated the need to iron close to the range or fireside in hot weather, and their constant temperatures prevented burns. However the most radical potential of these products, to decentralize the organization of the kitchen away from the control of the cook laboring at the range, was not developed. The range was an emotive fixture, recalling the cooking fire of ancient dwellings. It was set within a tiled recess like a fireplace and, in spite of the attendant inefficiencies, it was designed to show an area of open fire in the center so that the homely comforts of the fireplace would be felt even in the most utilitarian kitchen. "In the English view a fire-place is the one thing that gives life to the room and makes existence in it tolerable."[34]

Muthesius observed that the higher culinary arts were practically nonexistent in the English kitchen. Vegetables were always boiled, sauces were bought in bottles (he gave Worcester sauce as an example), and roast beef and mutton were served up alternately night after night so that the most distinguishing feature of English cooking, he believed, was its monotony. Unsophisticated palates were satisfied by rudimentary cooking methods; the open fire of the range was favored not only for toasting bread for breakfast, held out on a toasting fork, but also for roasting joints of meat, which were suspended and turned by a simple mechanism in front of a roasting fire. Ovens were arranged to either side and, in a large kitchen, the range had several ovens for bread and pastry as well as warming drawers and a grill. The hot water for the house as well as heat for cooking was provided by the range (although in houses with more than one bath, a separate boiler was recommended), and an iron rack for warming plates was built across the upper part of the fixture.

By the turn of the century this archaic cooking apparatus should, in any rational household, have been obsolete. The "extravagant, inconvenient, and laborious kitchen range" was large and unwieldy to work at. Insensitive to the need for subtle and immediate variations in temperature, it heated the kitchen throughout the day in summer as well as winter, and the time and energy required to keep it in working order, raking out ashes, sweeping the soot from the flues, and polishing and black-leading was an incessant drain on household resources.[35] Gas stoves were available as well as electrical alternatives and they were adopted in many kitchens as a compact and efficient supplement to the range, but Muthesius observed that although the gas stove was an invaluable and popular addition to the kitchen, it was regarded as a makeshift or

ABOVE: American designers were more rational in their attitude to cooking smells than their British contemporaries. The Gamble House kitchen was planned as an efficient work space with a vast canopy over the range to extract the heat and smells from the room.

temporary expedient. "While fully recognising the advantages of the newcomer, the public is unwilling to break finally with ancient custom."[36]

Muthesius complained that the English kitchen was dowdy and disappointing in appearance and that the appliances had an antiquated air compared with their continental counterparts because the housewife never entered the service wing. Of all the rooms in the house, however, it was the one in which attitudes to service and domestic labor were most clearly polarized during the Arts and Crafts period. The aesthetics of the laboratory, prefiguring Modernism, developed in larger kitchens. Features included glass shelves, gleaming metal fixtures, and white tiled walls and floors where even the servants were unwelcome when they were not working in case they introduced "dust and dirt and bacteria into a room that should be kept as free as possible of all these evils."[37] Kitchens of this type were planned and described as domestic machines, "arranged like a modern factory, so that from the moment when the food is delivered like raw material at the tradesman's door it will pass along until it is delivered as the finished product into the dining room."[38] At the opposite extreme, *The Craftsman* promoted an image of the kitchen as "a more homelike room. . .the special realm of the housewife and the living room of the whole family."[39]

Ultimately, the styling and organization of the Arts and Crafts kitchen depended upon who was to live and work in it. As homeowners of modest means increased in number and housewives became more familiar with the physical work as well as the management of their kitchens, the utilitarian aesthetics of the room were superseded by an emphasis on "homely cheer." The picturesque elements of the housekeeper's room, the butler's pantry, the scullery, and the kitchen were reduced and reassembled into compact compositions with pretty glazed cupboards for china built-in and an array of polished pans and utensils quaintly hanging from dressers or hooks on the wall.

The bald efficiency of the cook's kitchen was complicated by nostalgia and a desire to maximize the decorative potential of traditional implements. The modern housewife was unlikely to be tempted by the prospect of working in factory conditions and so, paradoxically, Arts and Crafts designers condemned their clients to labor at the range rather than the electric oven. The ideal of the cottage or farmhouse kitchen with its traditional order and scrubbed wooden surfaces was dressed up and eulogized. A new philosophy of service was written into the poetry of the simple life, so that the hours spent polishing pans, washing curtains, and raking out the range fire could be properly enjoyed.

Homemaking was revered as "one of the sacred tasks of life," and in Charles Keeler's *The Simple Home*, housework was redefined to seem both sexy and sacrosanct at the same time.[40] Service, according to Keeler, was the salvation of the individual: "Service is love realized in activity. The very mark which distinguishes love from lust."[41] Keeler described the home as a temple "consecrated to love" in which the form of worship was service and the high priestess, "the one who makes the supreme sacrifice, the one who has the supreme reward," was the housewife.[42] "The idea of woman's rights becomes insignificant in the face of this great privilege of service."[43] Intellectual arguments were

RIGHT: Boot scraper at Rodmarton Manor.

not the only, or even the most powerful, forces that persuaded women to gradually accept the duties which, in more affluent homes, had formerly belonged to their servants. The Arts and Crafts Movement was underpinned by patriarchal attitudes, rooted in Ruskin's philosophy, which sanctified the labor-intensive drudgery of the kitchen rather than subjecting it to progressive reform.[44]

The Craftsman conjured up images of the farmhouse kitchen and dining room combined. It boasted that the Craftsman kitchen with its hooded range was "one of the best aired and sunniest of all the rooms in the house."[45] Kitchens did become living spaces in many smaller Craftsman houses, furnished with outdoor porches. But the modern conveniences which were proudly listed as "almost unbelievable a generation ago," were limited to electric lighting, hot and cold running water, open plumbing, and "laundry conveniences"—which appear from illustrations to have consisted of a boiler rather than an open fire to heat the water and a built-in sink.

Keeler promoted a simpler standard of living so that men could be free from the demands of materialism, "rushing and jostling with the crowd in the scramble for wealth," and so enjoy a deeper and more fulfilling life. His text was exactly contemporary with that of Charlotte Perkins Gilman, one of the rare published voices of feminine dissent which exposes the hypocrisy of the Arts and Crafts ideal.

"We may all have homes to love and grow in without the requirement that half of us shall never have anything else. . .the thousands upon thousands of women, who work while life lasts to serve that sanctuary by night and day—to all these it may not be unwelcome to suggest that the home need be neither a prison, a workhouse, nor a consuming fire."[46] Gilman argued that women in their millions were marching out of their homes to find fulfilment in their daily work. "To work to the full capacity of one's powers is necessary for human development. . .No normal human mind can find full exercise in dusting the parlour and arranging the flowers; no, nor in twelve hours of nerve-exhaustion in the kitchen."[47] In the Arts and Crafts kitchen, however, design and philosophy were stacked in Keeler's favor.

CHAPTER SEVEN

COLD BATHS AND DRESSING IN THE BEDROOM

LEFT: One of the bedrooms at Rodmarton Manor with an oak bed by Sidney Barnsley set beneath a half tester designed and crafted by the estate staff. The bedroom table and chest were designed by Ernest Barnsley for his own use.

EX WAS EXCLUDED FROM nineteenth-century etiquette manuals, and novelists of the period left the antics of lovers to the reader's imagination long before the couples reached the bedroom. Nevertheless, sexual etiquette was an important factor in the design of the Arts and Crafts bedroom. Muthesius hinted darkly at the dire consequences of men and women encountering one another in a state of undress before they had prepared themselves, in private, for the night or the day ahead: "Only in the most primitive living-conditions do the man and woman dress in the same room. . .we need hardly labour the point." He also stressed the importance of arranging the door so that it opened away from the bed "to avoid embarrassing situations" when the maid arrived with an early morning cup of tea.[1]

The master bedroom, paradoxically, was the mistress' domain: "The bedroom belongs essentially to the woman and it might almost be said that the man merely enters it as her guest, as we have seen him doing in the drawing-room."[2] It was decorated and furnished as an intimate feminine space with a much smaller adjoining dressing room for the master of the house. Health and hygiene rather than sensuality dominated the design of the room and, although fantasy and romance became fashionable in the Arts and Crafts bedroom, there were no visual allusions to sex. Unlike their Art Nouveau contemporaries, who exploited the potential of paganism and decadence to titillate or disturb, Arts and Crafts designers and their clients were committed to the aesthetics of innocence and moral purity.

Female sexuality was only acceptable, socially, as a serene and passive force. Respectable women were revered for their quiet, unassuming wisdom. Their perception in spiritual matters, in issues of conscience and morality, was held in esteem, but "nice" women were neither worldly nor assertive, and their physical presence was always chaste and restrained. There was "an abysmal difference between the women one loved and respected and those one enjoyed—and pitied" and, although paintings by Rossetti, Moreau, and Klimt and the graphics of Aubrey Beardsley describe the femme fatale as a subject of fascination throughout the Arts and Crafts period, such women were dangerously associated with death and emasculation.[3] In the novels of Henry James and Edith Wharton the sophisticated culture of Europe was portrayed as a threat to the upright and unsullied values of the brave New World, and society conspired, in both Britain and America, to blame the indiscretions of its men folk on the irresistible charms of sexually provocative women. "All the elderly ladies. . .regarded any woman who loved imprudently as necessarily unscrupulous and designing, and mere simpleminded man as powerless in her clutches."[4]

As a consequence, the brief for the Arts and Crafts bedroom could not depend upon the adage that form follows function. The creation of a feminine domain in which sex, birth, and death—all occurrences that were surrounded, in Victorian culture, by elaborate rituals and taboos—were relatively commonplace, calling for tactical evasions and discretion. The Arts and Crafts bedroom was designed, therefore, to sanctify the restorative qualities of sleep and to accommodate the daily rituals of washing and dressing. The bed was emphatically a place of rest.

The Victorian bedroom had been stripped back and subjected to a stringent cleansing campaign from the 1870s so that Arts and Crafts designers faced two extreme forms of precedent. The first of these was the old-fashioned, unreformed nineteenth-century bedroom dominated by massive mahogany furniture—"heavy, ugly, and gloomy"—with a four-poster piled high with straw, hair, and wool mattresses surmounted by a feather bed. Velvet drapery or "smothering folds of dusty damask" enveloped the occupant, "while curtains to match trailed from beneath a huge gilt cornice above the window."[5] As Victorian physicians began to associate confined and airless living and working conditions with fatal diseases such as tuberculosis, these ornate interiors were condemned, and a crusade for more sanitary sleeping conditions decontaminated the bedroom, eliminating every superfluous detail of comfort and style. Design critics were too discreet to name the causes of bad smells in the bedroom (the practice of keeping a chamber pot under the bed persisted well into the twentieth century, even in houses with indoor lavatories), but Lady Barker deliberately shocked her readers in the first chapter of *The Bedroom and Boudoir* (published in 1878) by declaring that very few bedrooms were furnished and built "to remain thoroughly *sweet*, fresh and airy all through the night."[6] Incurable contagious diseases, high fevers, and

LEFT: Built-in bedroom furniture was invented by the Arts and Crafts Movement. Most clothes were laid flat rather than hung from rails and too many clothes stored in the bedroom were considered a health hazard.

RIGHT: Light, chintz curtains became fashionable in the Arts and Crafts home because they were pretty and easily washed. Hung with rings from a metal or wooden pole they replaced the heavy theatrical effects of Victorian drapery.

prolonged periods of illness were common in the late nineteenth century. Serious illnesses as well as mild afflictions were nursed at home, and it was widely believed that the cleanliness of the bedroom and the ability to disinfect its entire contents could be a matter of life or death. Ventilation and cleanliness, as a consequence, were the twin peaks which modern Victorian bedrooms aspired to achieve; although the Arts and Crafts Movement deliberately compromised these standards, the clinical demands of medical science remained a priority.

The Arts and Crafts bedroom negotiated a delicate balance between the physical requirements for sanitary surroundings needed in the sick room and a demand for more relaxed and comfortable interiors. Paneled walls and cupboards were painted white, "the colour of immaculate cleanliness," to show every speck of dirt.[7] Fitted carpets were banished and wooden floors were left bare or covered with small rugs (by the bed, the fireplace, and the clothes cupboard) which could be shaken outside every day. And "an hour or two's exposure to the air and sunshine will purify them [the rugs] greatly, after the beating and shaking has done its share."[8] Fireplaces were kept clear for ventilation, and every morning the windows and doors were opened wide "to secure a good current of air."[9] Medical recommendations that curtains should be abolished in the bedroom proved unpopular, but Arts and Crafts curtains in general, and bedroom curtains in particular, were simpler and more lightweight than their Victorian predecessors. Thin muslin curtains, replacing more elaborate laces, were hung across the lower lights of the bedroom window for privacy, and washable chintzes, patterned to complement the decoration of the walls, were widely used.

Short curtains, hung by metal rings from thin brass rods, were fashionable in Arts and Crafts homes; they were often set within the window recess in straight, ungathered widths so that there was no need for a pelmet. Greased rods harbored dust and grime but by rubbing the top and back of a well-dusted pole with a dry cake of black lead, readers of *The House* were advised that "the curtains will pull back and forward with a freedom that will be astonishing."[10] In exceptionally tall windows, such as those at Rodmarton, the upper and lower lights were separately hung with identical curtains so that they could be drawn or left open independently. Plain roller blinds, set between the curtain and the glass were used throughout the Arts and Crafts home to block out unwanted light. When they were fully rolled up, they were almost invisible, but Muthesius observed that, in spite of their usefulness, "They have a certain unalterable air of impoverishment and are totally lacking in artistic quality."[11]

The science of psychology was in its infancy during the Arts and Crafts period, but the benefits of a light, artistically decorated bedroom over the austerity of the Victorian sick room or the "dull, overcrowded, stuffy room where there is neither light, air, nor colour to lift up the feelings" were avidly promoted.[12] Rest was prescribed as a remedy for every kind of nervous and emotional disorder in the nineteenth century, and the bedroom was designed to induce an effect of calm and repose. The walls were often whitewashed or painted a plain color and, where wallpapers were used, delicate floral motifs in pastel colors were favored. "A bedroom paper ought never to have a distinct, spotted pattern on it, lest, if you are ill, it should incite you to count the designs or should 'make faces at you.'"[13] Victorian designs of ribbon bows and high-handled baskets of flowers were dismissed as irritating to the invalid. In their place more coherent decorative schemes were devised, founded on the Arts and Crafts principal that a single idea should inform the design of every aspect of the room: the patterns and colors of the wall treatment were conceived as part of a harmonious totality.

Morris & Co. were the first decorators to popularize delicate and simple wallpaper patterns for the bedroom, complemented by washable chintz curtains and white or pale painted woodwork. Their block-printed patterns were more expensive than the roller-printed designs of their competitors, but they lasted better and remained in fashion longer, thus Morris patterns provide a key element within a range of different types of Arts and Crafts bedrooms. Muthesius described Morris as the father of modern wallpaper and, in fact, he was more influential than any other figure in reforming late Victorian taste. "Some of Morris's papers, such as the celebrated 'Daisy pattern' and particularly the 'Pomegranate pattern' are as popular with the public today as they were forty-five years ago, when they first appeared on the market; indeed, in the past ten years particularly, the demand has risen steeply because the desire for art is becoming ever more general."[14]

Many of Morris's decorative designs were modern interpretations of ancient embroideries and adaptations of medieval images borrowed from illuminated manuscripts housed in the South Kensington Museum (now the Victoria and Albert Museum). The four-poster bed at Kelmscott Manor, furnished with fine printed hangings beneath a simple pelmet was loosely based on a romanticized medievalism but the light, airy fabrics and the embroidered counterpane patterned with simple flowers and foliage describe a poetic approach to the bedroom as a dream place in

ABOVE: The north bedroom at Standen, with "Powdered" wallpaper designed by Morris in 1874. Margaret Beale and her daughters embroidered the fine hangings to a Morris design and they were displayed on either side of the drawing-room fireplace until, for conservation reasons, they were moved upstairs.

which freshness and cleanliness were exemplified, rather than jeopardized, by the use of textiles.

Machine-made metal bedsteads "with great unmeaning blotches of 'pebble and splash' in cast brass" offended the sensibilities of Arts and Crafts designers.[15] Voysey disliked them for their tawdry glitter and their cold, inhospitable surfaces. "The proper ventilation of the bedroom and healthy conditions of rest do not entirely depend on air space or metal bedsteads. Indeed, the old fourposter was much more calculated to inspire right thoughts and feelings, and in a properly ventilated bedroom is as healthy and clean as any metal atrocity."[16] The four-poster bed, he suggested, offered a sense of protection and gave the bedroom an air of solemnity and importance. Iron and brass beds, nevertheless, were indispensable to the hygiene-conscious home owner until the late 1890s. When Webb planned the bedroom furniture for Standen with the Beales in 1893 he anticipated metal bedsteads and they were purchased from Heal's. It was not until 1897 when that firm introduced a range of wooden beds with iron lath frames that the sanitary status of the metal bed could be matched by designs which were "simple, quaint, and exceptionally pleasing in style" and the bed could be reinstated as "the soul of the bedroom."[17]

ABOVE: Wooden beds were considered unhygienic until Heal's revolutionized their design in 1897. This example was designed by W. R. Lethaby as part of a suite of oak bedroom furniture about a year later.

The clarity and light simplicity of the bedrooms at Standen are characteristic of an intermediary period in the design of the Arts and Crafts bedroom, before the acceptance of oak and ash bedsteads generated a fashion for complete bedroom suites with pale wood frames and art metal hinges and handles. Webb did not presume to specify the free-standing furniture for Standen, limiting his involvement to discreet suggestions and possibly a shopping expedition to Heal's with Mrs. Beale. The position of the beds, though, and all the permanent details of the room—from the sizes of the wardrobes to the styling of the fireplaces—came under his jurisdiction. These were designed to either defy or conform to the conventions of the period.

A southeasterly orientation, enjoying the morning sunshine without the heat of the sun in the late afternoon, was considered ideal for the principal bedrooms, and ancient customs as well as health and convenience were taken into account in the arrangement of each piece of furniture. It was traditional, according to Muthesius, for a woman to sleep to the left of her husband; when she woke it was appropriate for her side of the bed to be closest to the dressing table, which in turn was always near the window or arranged underneath it. The bed head was set against the wall with the bed projecting into the room so that air would circulate freely around the sleeper "whereas it easily stagnates in a corner."[18] It was considered bad planning to position the fireplace and the door to the man's dressing room so that the "extremely disagreeable" prospect of a bed with its foot to the window was unavoidable.[19] "The light streaming into the room on a summer morning is too precious to shut out entirely, but full upon one's face it is not conducive to a pleasant awakening."[20] The correctly positioned bed, therefore, had its head against a side wall with the window to the left and the door to the dressing room to its right. Good taste dictated that the bed covers should be thrown well back in the mornings so that the bed was aired before the house maid came to make it. The blankets, sheets, and mattress were regularly removed in order that the iron laths of the base of the bed and every ledge and crevice of the frame could be disinfected with a rag dipped in paraffin.

Only "eminently dustable" furniture was appropriate for the bedroom, and the Arts and Crafts period replaced the ponderous Victorian wardrobe, behind which germs of every description were suspected of lurking, with built-in cupboards designed to the clients' specifications.[21] Webb liaised with his clients' daughters as well as discerning the requirements for the master bedroom, promising Amy Beale that he would include as many of her requests in the wardrobe for her Larkspur bedroom at Standen as the space would allow—including the looking glass in the door.[22] One critic noted that the mirror undermined the unity of the paneled surface: "A better practice is to place the mirror on the inside of the door, which can be hinged so as to open at the proper angle for use"—but he allowed that at Standen, the client rather than the architect may have been responsible.[23]

The clothes cupboard was divided into compartments with shelves and drawers for hats, blouses, and boots. Only a third of the space was devoted to hanging dresses and skirts which were protected in cotton dust bags, buttoned down the front. "Mantles, bodices, and waistcoats should never be hung. They should be neatly folded, so as to keep them as straight and even as may be, and laid flat on a shelf."[24] Muthesius warned that fitted cupboards which stopped short of the ceiling were no better than free-standing wardrobes as repositories for dust, but Webb's sense of fitness for purpose (his client would have been unable to reach a shelf just below ceiling height), and his insistence on balanced proportions determined the height of the Standen cupboards. They were designed to extend the joinery around the fireplace, and the juncture was deliberately awkward to articulate the different functions of the paneled cupboard and the paneled fire surround.

The principal bedrooms at Standen were decorated with Morris & Co. wallpapers, white-painted woodwork, and boarded floors, covered with rugs. White lace and embroidered bedspreads accentuated the delicate purity of the beds, and the tile surrounds to each individually designed fireplace were white. Webb and his

BELOW: Washstand by Collinson and Lock and slop bucket in the Willow bedroom at Standen.

RIGHT: Ice-cold baths by the fireside and hot water summoned by maid-service for the washstand prevailed even in the most progressive Arts and Crafts bedrooms and dressing rooms. Although Standen was equipped with a modern bathroom, each of the bedrooms was furnished with a hip-bath and washstand en suite.

contemporaries R. N. Shaw and E. S. Nesfield reformed the design of bedroom fireplaces by first drawing the simple cast-iron grates which they required for their houses, then persuading manufacturers to produce them.[25] By the turn of the century, a considerable range of stylishly simple and economic grates were available from enterprising metalworkers in Britain and America. These either could be set directly into the chimney breast or, as at Standen, surrounded by plain or patterned tiles framed within a wooden surround. In the coordinated Arts and Crafts bedroom, they were designed to match the splash-back tiles to the washstand, but they had a practical as well as an aesthetic purpose: "The luster which is upon them reflects the light and warmth thrown out from the grate, and so considerably increases the heat of the fire. Add to this important utilitarian advantage the extremely tasteful appearance which they present and the ease with which they are cleansed, and I think they need no further attempt to justify their presence."[26]

The general arrangement of the Arts and Crafts bedroom, as well as each of its details, was meticulously planned to serve a succession of different functions throughout the day. In the morning, the mistress of the house remained in the master bedroom after her husband had retired to his dressing room and the room was furnished with a washstand and dressing table for her toilette. Men were expected to wash, dress, and undress in their dressing rooms; although purpose-built bathrooms were relatively commonplace in Arts and Crafts homes, the washstand, with its bowl and pitcher of hot water brought by the maid, prevailed. (With plumbing improvements later in the twentieth century it graduated to the anachronism of a built-in hand basin tucked into the corner of the room.[27]) It would have been considered unseemly for a man and woman to wash together in the bedroom so the dressing room was furnished with its own washstand close to the fireplace.

Only one bathroom served the twelve first-floor bedrooms for the Beale family and their guests at Standen. The difficulties of providing adequate supplies of hot water, necessitating an independent boiler, persuaded British architects and their clients that more than one bathroom, even in a large house, was unnecessary and extravagant. It was easier and more economical to install a system of bells to summon the maid whenever water was required.

A morning bath, nevertheless, was strongly recommended as a daily tonic: "The majority of people in fair health and vigour, either are or would be the better for the daily

use of a bath—cold in summer, and only slightly dashed with warm water even in winter. It is marvellous the difference a morning bath makes to those who can stand it."[28] Because the bathroom could only be used by one person at a time, portable hip baths, taken in front of the fire in the bedroom or dressing room and requiring minimal quantities of hot water, were popular. The most stalwart used a shallow sponging tin with a large sponge and a pitcher or bowl of freezing water. "To most people the sponging-tin seems to give sharper work, and to afford the greatest reaction, which is the main thing about a daily cold bath. This is, of course, greatly assisted by a really rough Turkish towel."[29]

Conditions in the bathroom were considerably more luxurious. The room was designed as "an inviting place in which to linger," and a plentiful supply of hot water was regarded as essential to the perfect bath.[30] Hot baths, however, were "for the 'Saturday night's wash,' so to speak," taken as an addition rather than alternative to the

LEFT: Arts and Crafts architects favored a cottage-style simplicity in the design of oak bathroom furniture which, in England, was neither stained nor varnished.

BELOW: Demonic shower devices squirted horizontal jets of hot and cold water as well as dousing the bather from above.

bracing morning bath.[31] The Arts and Crafts Movement redeemed the bathroom as a stylish rather than an entirely functional interior. Marble finishes were reserved for the most extravagant bathrooms; the walls were more usually tiled or finished with hard-polished plaster which could easily be wiped clean. Where the tiling was not taken up to the ceiling, it was often treated as a dado reaching to a height of around four feet six inches; the walls and ceiling above were painted with a waterproof oil-based paint.

The aesthetics of the bathroom were studied in their simplicity. Vivid tiles and richly grained and colored marbles were avoided and applied decoration was considered inappropriate: "A man in his pyjamas, or just out of them, is apt to look incongruous in the midst of much elaboration and though none may witness his discomfiture, yet it is well to avoid it."[32] White walls were preferred "so that by contrast our bodies may appear ruddy with health," and the bathroom fittings were always white to demonstrate their cleanliness.[33] Tiled floors were often fitted with a central gully-hole and arched ceilings were recommended so that condensation would run smoothly down the walls and away through the floor. However, the Arts and Crafts bathroom was not designed to be cold: "The bathroom should be heated and ventilated—in the smaller bathroom a towel-airer will serve to heat, and in larger ones a radiator may be added, as well as an open fireplace. For sheer unadulterated luxury nothing can be compared to the enjoyment of jumping out from a cold bath and dressing in front of a good fire."[34]

"Shower-baths" were the height of fashion in the Arts and Crafts bathroom. They were attached to the head of the bath and screened by a curtain or half-cylindrical zinc surround. Cold showers were encouraged as "refreshing and strengthening" at the end of a hot bath, and more elaborate free-standing showers were becoming increasingly popular at the turn of the century.[35] Designed to spray the bather from every direction, the overhead "rain-bath" was supplemented by sprays of different temperatures and intensities down the sides, including "needle" and "wave" sprinklers, with the inevitable cold spray below the waist and a fountain squirting upward from the base. Cast-iron and earthenware baths were the most commonly used. An Arts and Crafts affinity for wood meant that they were often enclosed by paneling—although this was discouraged on the grounds of good hygiene. A hand basin, a heated towel-rail, a mirror, and shelves and dishes for washing implements completed the furnishing of the bathroom. The Victorian practice of including a lavatory in a small adjoining room was reviled as totally inadmissible and barbarous. "Even in its most splendid form, a lavatory is an appliance that one would prefer to keep out of sight as far as possible. . .its presence evokes unpleasant associations of ideas, even assuming that the closet is entirely odourless, which can never be taken for granted."[36]

BELOW: Voysey's own single bed with bedside table and towel rail.

RIGHT: Washstand and towel rail designed by W. R. Lethaby.

Muthesius believed that the turn-of-the-century bathroom would be regarded by future generations as the most eloquent expression of the age. The immaculate white surfaces of tiled walls and floors, the functional new forms of glazed stoneware baths and hand basins supported by chrome or nickel-plated legs and frames, with gleaming metal faucets, soap and sponge dishes, achieved an absence of sentimentality and "studied atmospheric qualities" which he identified as the foundation of modern architecture and design. "A modern bathroom. . .is like a piece of scientific apparatus, in which technique of a high intellectual order rules, and if any 'art' were dragged in it would merely have a disturbing effect." [37] The ingenious and uncompromisingly modern innovations in the bathroom, however, had little or no effect on the washing facilities which prevailed in the dressing room and bedroom.

Hip baths were removed from view when they were not in use but the washstand was a permanent requirement in the bedroom, and it was invariably designed with a dressing table to match: "these pieces always form a pair. . .and their form shows that they belong together." [38] Colored wash basins and pitchers with mottled glazes were made fashionable by the Arts and Crafts Movement, replacing more delicate white porcelain models with painted decorations, and the equipment on the wash stand's tiled or marble surface was completed by a soap dish, a sponge dish, and a toothbrush container. A screen of gathered fabric which could easily be removed for washing protected the walls above the splashback of more elaborate washstands, towel rails were fastened to the sides, and a cupboard or shelf was provided for chamber pots or boots below. The simplest Arts and Crafts washstands, designed by artists and architects such as Ford Madox Brown, Lethaby, and Voysey, were reduced to their most rudimentary forms and the functions of washing and drying were separated. They dispensed with the distraction of colored tile or marble surfaces, insisting upon a cottage simplicity in the design of painted deal and scrubbed oak pieces which depended for their effect entirely upon their forms and proportions.

Every bedroom, including that of the maid, was furnished with a dressing table where women attended to their hair and selected their jewelry. Designed as a table, with drawers below for small or delicate items of clothing, and furnished with a tilting mirror, it was positioned under the window to benefit from the best daylight. A second, full-length mirror was provided for dressing. Miniature drawers were sometimes designed into the piece to hold jewelry, and convention demanded that the dressing-table top should be arranged as the quintessence of feminine delicacy. An "elegant little cloth" was laid across its wooden surface and a long tray of silver, tortoiseshell, or fine wood contained a set of brushes and combs with a handmirror of the same material.

The formality of the arrangement was both intimate and impersonal because women guests were invited into the master bedroom when they attended balls and other evening entertainments, and the dressing table was placed at their disposal. Outside their own homes, ladies did not remove their hats during the day under any circumstances. In evening dress, however, they were invited to leave their coats and cloaks in the hostess' bedroom, and the dressing table was used to perfect their elaborately pinned-up hairstyles. Young women began to wear their hair up as a sign of sexual maturity, when they graduated to full-length dresses. Long loose hair, as Rossetti's paintings and Debussy's *Pelléas et Mélisande* describe, was highly charged as a fetishist emblem of

ABOVE: Morris wallpaper and fabrics were combined with walnut furnishings by Isaac Scott in the Glessner House master bedroom. Victorians believed that it was unhealthy to read in bed and in modern bedrooms an upright sofa or daybed was provided but the Glessners preferred a more traditional chaise longue.

female sexuality; from adolescence onward women only let their hair down within the privacy of the bedroom.

Flowers were frequently sent as tokens of esteem and affection at the turn of the century and small, personal bouquets were arranged on the dressing table. Newland Archer, the hero in Edith Wharton's *The Age of Innocence,* every morning sent a box of flowers symbolizing bridal purity to his betrothed, who exclaimed: "It's so delicious—waking every morning to smell lilies-of-the-valley in one's room!"[39] Arts and Crafts ceramicists produced exquisite small vases for single stems but large bouquets were avoided and stale flowers were believed to be "absolutely poisonous in a sleeping-room."[40] Scent bottles were well sealed or corked for similar reasons: "Inhaling scents while you are asleep will often produce nausea, which, with some people turns to actual sickness."[41]

The dressing room was the gentleman's domain, furnished with its own fitted cupboards and chests of drawers as well as a dressing table and long mirror. It was not unusual to find a single bed in the dressing room, ostensibly for late nights and early morning starts, and the room was decorated with a functional simplicity: "It is but a dressing and sleeping apartment, in which the owner never thinks of sitting or living. For such uses the plainness of asceticism seems most desirable."[42] In larger houses the master bedroom was furnished with two dressing rooms. At the Glessner House in Chicago, Richardson designed a pair of dressing rooms for his clients so that, as an enclave away from the spaces where house guests were regularly entertained, the master bedroom became a comfortable sitting room where the Glessners could relax before dinner, without the distractions of washing and dressing facilities. Frances Glessner's dressing room was more spacious than that of her husband, and both rooms were sandwiched, side by side, between the bedroom and their private bathroom. John Glessner's dressing room opened directly onto the bedroom corridor, as well as the bedroom and the bathroom, so that his valet could attend to his needs and he could arrive and leave without disturbing his wife. Her dressing room was enclosed within the corner of the plan, however, and could be reached only through the bedroom.[43]

Men's clothes, it was believed, kept their shape better if they were laid flat rather than hung up. Thus the dressing room was furnished with a tallboy or a clothes cupboard comprising drawers beneath a cupboard with pull-out shelves where suits were laid out. Trousers were folded with their four seams exactly aligned, effectively pressing the creases to front and back, and coats, waistcoats, and shirts were carefully folded. Both men and women changed their clothes frequently during the day and different suits were required for business, for wearing about the house, and for dinner. Special outfits were worn for tennis, cycling, and other sports, and the dress code for the country was different from that of the town. It was considered injudicious, however, to keep an enormous store of suits and garments of the same kind. "People who dress well at a moderate expense never do this. They have what they need, bestow good care upon their belongings, and mend them when necessary. . .Fashionable garments very soon get out of date, and the more 'stylish' they were when new, the more remarkable they seem when the mode has altered."[44] Maintaining large stocks of underwear, in particular, was regarded as an anxiety—"They need constantly looking after, or they deteriorate in condition"—and changes in physique were cited as a likely source of "many disappointments."[45]

Aside from the need to change their clothes, women returned to the bedroom throughout the day, particularly in houses where there was no morning room or boudoir. "In many cases a woman's bedroom is a sitting room as well. Here she will sew and read and even entertain her intimates, and spend, perhaps, more time than in any other one room of her house."[46] It was often furnished with a desk where she could read and write letters and, later in the day, where her diaries were kept. Her closest women friends, who called singly in the mornings, could be entertained in the privacy of the bedroom. In addition, the custom of dressing for dinner every evening meant that in many households it was an intimate domestic space where family members could relax or exchange confidences before they joined their guests in the drawing room. Because reading in bed was considered unhealthy, a Victorian affection for daybeds and chaise longues arranged across the foot of the bed in front of the fireplace, continued in many Arts and Crafts homes. In the master bedroom at the Glessner House, William Morris wallpapers and fabrics were combined with a red velvet chaise longue "for casual 'lying downs' through the day."[47] The elegant contours and soft upholstered curves of the Victorian chaise longue were more often replaced in the Arts and Crafts bedroom, however, by the upright form of the Queen Anne sofa or the unyielding oak frame of the daybed.

The importance of good ventilation in the bedroom, and the need to "turn the room out" and clean underneath and behind every item of furniture, discouraged the Arts and Crafts propensity to rationalize and unify the different elements within the room by building all the furniture in. Muthesius complained of anxieties over making splashes and a general lack of elbow room where washstands were built into recesses; he also questioned the desirability of sleeping in rooms surrounded on two or three sides by cupboards crammed full of clothes which were only emptied and aired infrequently. At the Gamble House in Pasadena, California, the planning of the bedrooms and their furniture exemplified a more versatile approach, in which fine materials and exquisite design detailing by Greene and Greene were compatible with the most advanced medical theories. The Greenes' father was a physician specializing in respiratory diseases so that the importance of a free flow of air in sleeping rooms—where their clients would spend between seven and ten hours of every day—was a priority in their work. Badly designed houses were cited as a cause of consumption at the turn of the century. Although in most Arts and Crafts homes the practice of sleeping with the windows open regardless of the weather (merely adjusting the amount of the opening in the winter) was regarded as adequate for ventilation purposes, a vogue for sleeping outdoors on open porches was highly recommended by physicians "as a nerve sedative and as a tissue builder for the lungs."[48]

In Greene and Greene's Californian holiday houses the sleeping porch was an attractive alternative to the generous bedroom accommodation which the Greenes habitually provided. In the Gamble House every member of the family had access to a sheltered outdoor room, positioned to take advantage of the most favorable breezes drifting from the north and west across the orange groves of the Arroyo Seco. Because it served as a winter home, the Gamble House porches were often cool. The claims concerning the therapeutic properties of sleeping porches, however, led to an almost fanatical enthusiasm for the benefits of sleeping outside, even in freezing conditions. Thus houses by Lutyens and Voysey in Berkshire and Surrey, England, were furnished with brick sleeping porches beneath tiled hipped roofs, adapting vernacular traditions to a thoroughly modern ideal. It was believed that colds could not be caught out of doors, and that children's diseases, in particular, could be prevented or cured by sleeping outside. "Pure air bathing the lungs eight or nine hours each night cannot fail to work wonders upon either real or fancied ills. It exterminates a crusty temper and irritable nerves; it develops the appetite; it cures insomnia; it repairs the respiratory organs; it creates a wealth of cheerfulness, and so a better view of life."[49] For the most ascetic Arts and Crafts clients, however, the combination of extreme austerity with

physical discomfort—requiring an acclimatization period of several months of staunch perseverance and sleepless nights—had a subliminal appeal. It was bound to be beneficial almost by virtue of its unpleasantness.

Sleeping out was not for the fainthearted (although sufferers from rheumatism and neuralgia were encouraged, provided that they protected themselves from the wind and dew). Nor was it to be contemplated lightly in a spirit of adventure. Hammocks were confined to the attic and in their place permanent beds fitted with castors were recommended, with a canopy of dark material suspended from the porch ceiling and attached to a hoop over the bed to protect the head and screen the sleeper from the light of the rising sun. The canopy was thrown back, naturally, for most of the night and the assiduous Arts and Crafts client rose with the sun. Thermal nightcaps, worn in layers, were de rigueur in colder climates but additional blankets were thought unnecessary: "People sleeping out grow to require surprisingly little bedding as the blood gradually thickens."[50] The Gamble House porches were designed as raised terraces furnished with rattan armchairs and recliners for daytime and evening, as well as for sleeping out at night. Enclosed by long timber rails and sheltered beneath low pitch and elaborately

ABOVE: The master bedroom at the Gamble House decorated in unfashionably dark, earth colors. The door on the left opens onto the sleeping porch while that on the right leads to a small en suite bathroom.

constructed timber roofs, essential to the aesthetics of the exterior, they were cunningly planned so that Mary Gamble could oversee all the antics of her two teenage boys while her own sleeping porch and that of her resident sister, "Aunt Julia," were shielded by the contours of the building to afford areas of absolute privacy.

The Gamble House bedrooms were designed and furnished by the Greenes as complete interiors which combine elegance and refinement with spacious simplicity and airiness. All of the principal bedrooms were arranged with windows or with doors to the sleeping porches on two or more walls for cross-ventilation. Walk-in closets in the master bedroom and the ground-floor guest room obviated the need for an insanitary assortment of clothing close to the sleeping quarters. There are no dressing rooms at the Gamble House, which would have been superfluous in Aunt Julia's room and the boys' bedroom. Although American architects followed the plumbing innovations which their British contemporaries pioneered, they were less inhibited in their use of hot water. Five bathrooms serve the ground and first floor bedrooms at the Gamble House, removing the need for washstands in the bedrooms; the custom in smaller houses of using the bathroom as a gentleman's dressing room would have been adopted when necessary.

The use of ornament in the Gamble House bedrooms is intrinsic to the forms and fittings of essential furniture. Its delicate scale and subtle positioning, down the side of a mirror or across the face of a writing case, for example, is appropriate to the quiet, private situations in which the pieces were used. No ledges or heavily carved details that would harbor dust were permitted. However, in the ground floor guest room the bedheads are profiled, with a stepped curve which recurs as a motif throughout the house, and incised with fragile flowers and stems of climbing roses.

The guest room is the most conventional bedroom in the house, furnished with twin brass bedsteads, plated with nickel silver. It was customary for twin beds to be furnished with castors so that they could be pushed together as required and easily moved for cleaning purposes, but issues of hygiene were not permitted to dominate the aesthetics or use of materials in the Gamble House bedrooms. The quarter-sawn oak floor in the guest room is covered by a single pale green rug with a border patterned in darker green designed to tone with the muted colors of the plain painted walls. The Greenes considered each of their interior elevations as balanced compositions. The proportions of each wall: the height and width of skirtings and picture rails; the positions of the doors and windows; and the detailing of their panels and glazing bars were all individually designed to evoke a sense of unity and calm. Mahogany sconces inlaid with roses of finest silver wire support Tiffany glass lanterns in the guest room to cast a soft light over the beds, the dressing table, and the writing desk in the corner of the room. In contrast to English Arts and Crafts bedrooms, the subdued earth colors and lights were intended as a retreat from the relentless brilliance of California sunshine.

Mary Gamble was closely involved in specifying the furniture for each of the bedrooms. The distinction in style between the maple dressing table, writing desk, and chairs in the guest room and the furniture in her own master bedroom describes a breach between her bold personal taste and the standards which she imagined would please her visitors. The guest room furniture is lighter and more graceful than that of the master bedroom and, although it was exquisitely detailed with silver drawer pulls and inlays, it was significantly cheaper—less than half the cost of the black walnut furniture in the master bedroom. With the exception of a full-length mirror, fixed to the east wall adjacent to the windows, all of the pieces in the guest room are free-standing and their arrangement, with the dressing table and writing desk to either side of the long window, was both elegant and practical. The master bedroom, by comparison, was emphatically solid and dark. The standard acceptance of pale colors and feminine delicacy in the bedroom was dispensed with in favor of a more unorthodox vision of stillness and seclusion. Like the drawing room directly below, Mary Gamble's master bedroom was decorated and planned to dignify and rationalize routine procedures, mixing convention with an autocratic independence.

Although the master bedroom is positioned in the northwest corner of the plan, the windows are shaded from the heat of the afternoon sun by deep sheltering eaves to the west and a sleeping porch to the north. The walls are painted brown to tone with Port Orford cedar joinery and paneling and a beige ceiling and frieze—producing an effect of intimacy and warmth that made no concessions to contemporary trends. There is a creative disparity between the colors and brilliant light of the landscape which the bedroom and its porch were designed to survey and the somber earth tones of the interior. Mary Gamble's sleeping porch was originally furnished with a utilitarian metal bedstead but twin beds of black walnut ornamented with ebony and precious stones were designed as the ceremonial focus of the interior room. Floral patterns inlaid in the bed heads and carved reliefs encircling pierced motifs in the feet are asymmetrically designed so that they are only balanced, as a composition, when the beds are regarded together. The bed heads are set against the north wall of the room, flanked by doors to the bathroom and the porch to east and west respectively, and a single bedside table divides the pair. The position of a chiffonier close to the window in the southwest corner indicates that Mary Gamble slept to the right of her husband and, like the drawing room below, the four quarters of the room were each assigned a separate identity. The integrity of the interior as a single coherent space, nevertheless, is so meticulously balanced that the removal of a single piece of furniture would disrupt the harmonics of its composition.

A row of built-in cupboards, with a walk-in closet opposite, in the southwest corner of the room, furnished with its own small window, provided ideal conditions for the storing of clothes at the furthest extreme from the beds. "Hygienically speaking it would be far better to keep only the most essential clothing in the room itself and all the rest in a clothes-closet that can be aired, that is, a clothes-cupboard enlarged to the size of a room with a window to the outer air." [51] Between the closet and the window, which runs the entire length of the west wall, the chiffonier surmounted by a tilting mirror was designed so that instead of sitting at the more usual dressing table, Mary Gamble would have stood to attend to her hair. Her taste as a collector colored the decoration of the piece. Shades of blue and green, lifted from the iris decoration of one of her Rookwood vases inspired the ornamental inlays. In the opposite corner of the room the yellow dogwood flowers of a second vase were stylized and carved into the cupboard doors of a writing desk but these were private compliments. The carved doors to the interior compartments of the desk are revealed only when it is opened.

While the west side of the bedroom, freshened by cooling breezes from the windows and the porch door, was allocated to Mary Gamble's requirements for dressing and writing letters in the mornings and the beds were assigned to the north wall, the east side of the room, furthest from the windows, was designed as an intimate family space. A day bed was built-in to suggest an enclosure around the fireplace, with cedar shelves and

paneling to one side providing an ideal setting for the deep luminous tones of Mary Gamble's collection of Rookwood vases. Above the day bed, interior art-glass windows elaborate on the gold and ocher tones which recur throughout the room, and a single lantern, sketched in Charles Greene's notes as a "Bright light over seat for Mr G." supplements the sconces over the beds and the pendant lamps which light the room.[52] The interior window has a clandestine appeal, affording a view over the staircase and across the broad first floor landing to the guest bedrooms on the opposite side of the house, but it contributed, too, to the ventilation of the bedroom. Leaving open the door and external windows to the Gamble's bathroom, adjoining the northeast corner of the room, produced an additional cross-current of air.

It was usual to furnish the bedroom with two or three light chairs which could easily be moved for convenience, in addition to more comfortable seats in the master bedroom. Mary Gamble's workbook describes different combinations for each of the bedrooms. Her sons' room was furnished with sturdy Craftsman furniture (described as "Mission furniture" in Charles Greene's notes), but in all of the bedrooms, chairs which were designed for either general or particular purposes were united by a common style. Two rocking chairs were drawn up in front of the generous fireplace in the master bedroom. A low shoe chair was specially proportioned for fastening the many buttons and laces on the fashionable boots and shoes of the period, and three straight chairs were provided in addition to a chair for Mary Gamble's desk. They were clearly defined as integral components within the overall design of the master bedroom, however, by the pierced motif, derived from the symbolic form of a Japanese sword guard, and the ebony frame, which ornaments the beds and the chiffonier and recurs in the flaring form of the back splat of each chair.

The Gamble House bedrooms are characteristic of the Arts and Crafts Movement in their unique adaptation of standard conventions interspersed with rational innovations and symbolic or sentimental idiosyncrasies. They give little credence to Muthesius's claim that health and freshness in the bedroom dictated the use of white woodwork and cheerful colors "evocative of freshly laundered white linen, to which an aura of sunshine in the open air still clings."[53] It would be facile to imagine that because the walls were brown they were left dirty or undusted. The need for cleanliness and good ventilation informed every detail of the design, and where the aesthetic of cleanliness was imperative, in each of the Gamble House bathrooms, they were tiled and painted in white.

The brown walls of the master bedroom were daring, however, because they crossed the boundaries of sexual appropriation. The dark woods and plain, relatively robust forms that distinguish the room were traditional to the decoration of bachelor bedrooms and to dressing rooms, libraries, and dining rooms—masculine spaces within the house. The tall chiffonier, the businesslike desk, and the day-bed might as easily have been used by David Gamble as by Mary, and the memo concerning the reading lamp demonstrates that both parties were prone to "lying downs." It was Mary Gamble's taste, however, rather than that of her husband, which shaped the aesthetics of the room in collaboration with her architects and far from being diminished or negated by that process it was her self-assurance and preferences as a collector that inspired the design.

The master bedroom at the Gamble House concludes a trend in the design and decoration of the Arts and Crafts home toward unorthodox arrangements, politely couched in traditional forms and materials. The reactions of less enlightened home owners to the covert messages of a woman's bedroom bearing all the attributes of a masculine space are not recorded, but an absence of written documentation, like the censorship with which sex was surrounded, does not signify an absence of fact. Within the privacy of the bedroom, the ideals and the personalities of the clients could be more freely expressed than in any other room in the house, and the decoration and furnishing of the Gamble House bedroom suggests a stable and evenly balanced relationship between David and Mary Gamble, perceptively expressed through the Greenes' design.

The planning of every space in the Arts and Crafts home; the styling of each of the rooms; and the selection and detailing of the furniture, fabrics, and the decorative and functional objects, which contributed to the comfort and vitality of the interior, allude to ephemeral relationships and to forgotten routines. Houses which have been preserved without significant alterations and with their original decorative schemes and collections still in place are rare and, divorced from the personalities and the lifestyles which they were designed to serve, they can only account for the material realities of Arts and Crafts. Issues of meaning, the possibilities of an interior or a detail within it as a stylish negotiation—an intellectual or an emotional stance through which the rituals of daily life were allowed to express profound or political convictions—can only be recognized and reconstructed with research and imagination. And yet these very issues were central to the ambitions of the movement. Arts and Crafts enshrined the traditions that it upheld, celebrating the principles of honesty and simplicity. It embraced rational innovations in building and in lifestyle, but its most significant contribution to twentieth-century culture might be the freedom and agility with which it adapted the conventions of domestic design in order to arrive at a more flexible definition of the home as a sophisticated or an intuitive statement which interpreted the values, the habits, and the individuality of both client and designer.

■ NOTES ■

CHAPTER ONE

1 Edith Wharton, *The Age of Innocence*, set in the 1870s, first published in America by D. Appleton & Co., 1920, Penguin 1996 edition, p. 68.

2 Hermann Muthesius, *The English House*, first published by Wasmuth in Berlin, 1904–5, English translation, (Crosby Lockwood Staples, London, 1979,) p. 69.

3 C.F.A. Voysey, specification of work for White Cottage, 68 Lyford Road, London, 1903, private collection.

4 Wilde added a dash of Ruskin to the epigram: "have nothing in your houses that has not been a joy to the man who made it and is not a joy to those that use it." Oscar Wilde, *Essays and Lectures*, 3rd ed., Methuen & Co. Ltd., London, 1911, p. 190.

5 Clarence Cook, *The House Beautiful*, Charles Scribner's Sons, 1881, p. 19.

6 Los Angeles Investment Company, *Practical Bungalows. Typical California Homes, with Plans*, 1912, no pagination.

7 Advertisement feature: "Join the Craftsman Home-Builders' Club," *Country Life in America*, Vol. 5, 1903, p. 197.

8 Robert Judson Clark (ed.) *The Arts and Crafts Movement in America 1876–1916*, Princeton University Press, 1972.

9 The New York edition of *Building* for 1886 (Vol. 4), for example, includes lavish illustrations of English houses by Ernest George, William Burges, R. N. Shaw and others.

10 Quoted from a speech by William Morris of 1879, W. R. Lethaby, *Philip Webb and his Work*, Oxford University Press, Oxford, 1935, p. 149.

11 Lethaby, *Philip Webb*, p. 144.

12 There were more painters and sculptors than architects and designers among the Guild's initial membership, and it is remarkable that eminent painters like Alfred Parsons and the sculptors Onslow Ford, Sir George Frampton and Sir William Reynolds-Stephens, many of whom were more famous at the turn of the century than their architect contemporaries, have been expunged from histories of Arts and Crafts.

13 H.J.L.J. Massé, *The Art Workers' Guild 1884–1934*, Oxford, 1935, p. 23.

14 William Morris, "Art and the people: a socialist's protest against capitalist brutality; addressed to the working classes" (1883), published in May Morris, *William Morris, artist writer socialist*, first published 1936, 2nd ed. (Russell & Russell, New York, 1966), p. 383.

15 John Ruskin, *The Seven Lamps of Architecture*, first published 1880, George Allen ed. (London, 1904), p. 97.

16 Oscar Wilde, "House Decoration," initially given as a lecture on 11 May 1882 in America entitled "The Practical Application of the Principles of the Aesthetic Theory to Exterior and Interior House Decoration, With Observations upon Dress and Personal Ornaments." Published in *Oscar Wilde, Essays and Lectures*, 1908, 3rd. ed. (Methuen & Co. Ltd., London, 1911), p. 161.

17 This road building anecdote may have been a fiction, see Martin Fido, *Oscar Wilde*, Hamlyn, 1973, p. 28. It is recounted in Oscar Wilde, *Essays and Lectures*, pp. 193–4.

18 Oscar Wilde, *Essays and Lectures*, p. 177.

19 Walter Crane, "Of the revival of design and handicraft: with notes on the work of the Arts and Crafts Exhibition Society," published in *Members of the Arts and Crafts Exhibition Society, Arts and Crafts Essays*, Charles Scribner's Sons, New York, 1893, p. 10.

20 J. W. Mackail, *The Life of William Morris*, Vol. 2, first published 1899, 2nd ed. (Longmans, London, 1901) p. 200.

21 J. W. Mackail, *Life of William Morris*, Vol. 2, p. 197.

22 Ibid., p. 201.

23 Review of Morris & Co. shop, *Building News*, 1880.

24 John Ruskin, *The Seven Lamps of Architecture*, first published 1849, 1904 edition (George Allen, London), p. 13.

25 The furniture and fittings were supplied by Kendal Milne in Manchester.

26 Anon., "Some recent designs by Mr. C.F.A. Voysey," *The Studio*, Vol. 7, 1896, p. 209.

27 In October 1893 almost the entire issue of *The Studio* was devoted to a review of the London Arts and Crafts Exhibition. *The Studio* observed that the exhibition "attracts the classes rather than the masses" in spite of the Society's efforts and that its influence, as a consequence, would be gradual. Aymer Vallance, "The Arts and Crafts Exhibition Society at the New Gallery, 1893," *The Studio*, Vol. 2, 1893, pp. 3–27.

28 Lewis F. Day, quoted in "In Search of 'the Latest,'" *The House*, Vol. 1, 1897, pp. 29–30.

29 *The House*, Vol. 1, p. 1.

30 *The House*, Ibid.

31 Ibid., p. 187.

32 Charlotte Perkins Gilman, *The home, its work and influence*, William Heinemann, London, 1904, p. 12.

33 Ibid., p. 11.

34 John Ruskin, *Sesame and Lilies*, first delivered as a lecture in Manchester, 1864.

35 Her husband's involvement, if she was married, was often nominal beyond the design of the external shell and the overall cost of the project.

CHAPTER TWO

1 George Bernard Shaw, "Morris as I knew him" preface to May Morris, *William Morris, artist writer socialist*, Vol. 2, p. xx.

2 Letter from Dante Gabriel Rossetti to Jane Morris, 27 February 1878, quoted in John Bryson (ed.), *Dante Gabriel Rossetti and Jane Morris, Their Correspondence*, Clarendon Press, Oxford, 1976.

3 Hermann Muthesius, *The English House*, p. 17.

4 Hermann Muthesius, *The English House*, p. 135 and May Morris, (ed.), *The Collected Works of William Morris with introductions by his daughter May Morris*, Vol. 1, Longmans Green & Co., London, 1910, p. xxiv.

5 May Morris, *Collected Works*, Vol. 1, p. xxv.

6 May Morris, *William Morris, artist writer socialist*, Vol.1, p. 43.

7 When the loom rooms were transferred to Merton Abbey, the stables and coach house were used as a studio for big working drawings and later converted into a hall for socialist meetings held every Sunday evening.

8 May Morris, *Collected Works*, Vol. XIII, p. xvi.

9 Hermann Muthesius, *The English House*, p. 135.

10 George Bernard Shaw, *Love among the artists*, first published 1881, Constable & Co. edition, 1932, p. 224.

11 C.S.S. Johnson, "On building a house," *The House*, Vol. 1, 1897, p. 220.

12 Hermann Muthesius, *The English House*, p. 71.

13 Letter from Edwin Lutyens to Lady Emily, 1897, quoted in Christopher Hussey, *The Life of Sir Edwin Lutyens*, Country Life, London, 1953, p. 67. The Lutyens home and office remained at 29 Bloomsbury Square until the expiry of the lease in 1914.

14 May Morris, *Collected Works*, Vol. XIII, p. xviii.

15 Hermann Muthesius, Op. cit., p. 83.

16 George Bernard Shaw, "Morris as I knew him" preface to May Morris, *William Morris*, Vol. 2, p. xxiv.

17 "Standen Memories," unpublished typescript by James and Margaret Beale's grandchildren, National Trust archives, p. 5.

18 Ibid., p. 5.

19 Webb's second house, Arisaig in Scotland, designed in 1863, contained one of the earliest examples of a living hall, and although the idea gathered momentum in the 1870s among designers like R. N. Shaw, it was Webb who integrated the living hall fully into the discreetly progressive planning of his houses. See Sheila Kirk, *Philip Webb*, Academy Editions, 2000.

20 Hermann Muthesius, Op. cit., p. 89.

21 Helen Beale, one of Margaret and James's daughters, was renowned for her skill at billiards and snooker.

22 See Wendy Hitchmough, *Arts and Crafts Gardens*, Pavilion, 1997 for a more detailed analysis of the evolution and character of the Arts and Crafts garden.

23 Robinson admired the garden at Standen and sent a photographer to record it. Undated letter from William Robinson to Margaret Beale, West Sussex Record Office, Standen Ms. 251.

24 Letter from Aglaia Coronio to Margaret Beale, West Sussex Record Office, Standen Ms. 252.

25 "Standen Memories" p. 10. This anecdote is also recounted in Mark Girouard, "Standen," *Country Life*, Vol. cxlvii, 1970, pp. 494–7, 554–7. Helen Beale wrote to him to correct his information on the fee from 6d to 1d, West Sussex Record Office, Standen Ms. 245.

26 Hermann Muthesius, Op. cit., p. 86.

27 Lawrence Weaver, "Standen, East Grinstead, a residence of Mr. James S. Beale," *Country Life*. Vol. 27, 7 May 1910, p. 666.

28 Ibid., p. 670.

29 Lawrence Weaver, "Standen," p. 668.

30 Philip Webb, building specification for Standen, quoted in Oliver Garnett, *Standen*, The National Trust, 1993, p. 23.

31 Halsey Ricardo, writing "of houses in general, but with Standen especially in mind," quoted in Lawrence Weaver, "Standen," p. 668.

32 Ibid., p. 668.

33 Webb's specification shows that initially the red Keymer bricks were to have been used more extensively. Stock bricks were used in their place in order to avoid an effect that would have been too strident in color.

34 Lawrence Weaver, "Standen," p. 671.

35 1909 Housing and Town Planning Act, quoted in Donald Read, *Edwardian England 1901–15, society and politics*, George Harrap & Co. Ltd., 1972, London, p. 38.

36 Henry James, *The Europeans*, first published 1878, Penguin Popular Classics edition, 1995, p. 33.

37 Quoted in Marianna Griswold Van Rensselaer, *Henry Hobson Richardson and his works*, Houghton, Mifflin & Co., Boston and New York, 1888, p. 38.

38 Between June and September the Glessner family spent their summers at "The Rocks."

39 John Glessner, "The Story of a House," unpublished and undated manuscript written by Glessner for his children. Typescript in Glessner House archives, Chicago, p. 8.

40 The reading classes were inaugurated in 1894.

41 Frances Glessner, "Journal," 5 April 1885, Glessner House archives, Chicago.

42 John Glessner, "The Story of a House," p. 6.

43 Ibid., p. 14.

44 Ibid., p. 14.

45 Ibid., pp. 14–15. This account of architectural genius on tap is perhaps romanticized. Richardson repeatedly refined and remade the drawings for his buildings, and even when the construction was in progress he would alter the design: "If when it is begun it fails to look as it should, it is not only the architect's privilege but his duty to alter it in any way he can." The Glessner House was constructed after his death.

46 May Morris, *William Morris, artist writer socialist*, Vol. 1, p. 55.

47 Written account of the visit by Mr. Jaques, who worked in Richardson's office and accompanied him on his trip to England. Quoted in Marianna Griswold Van Rensselaer, *Henry Hobson Richardson*, p. 28.

48 Ibid., p. 28.

49 John Glessner, "The Story of a House," p. 12. Frances Glessner's embroideries to Morris's designs were donated to the Chicago Art Institute.

50 John Glessner, "The Story of a House," p. 14.

51 Ibid., p. 2.

Chapter Three

1 Hermann Muthesius, *The English House*, p. 81

2 C.F.A. Voysey, "Ideas in Things," in Raffles Davidson (ed), *The Arts Connected with Building: Lectures on craftsmanship and design, delivered at Carpenter's Hall, London Wall, for the Worshipful Company of Carpenters*, Batsford, London, 1909, p. 130.

3 C.F.A. Voysey, "The English Home," *The British Architect*, Vol. LXXV, 1911, p. 70.

4 Ibid., p. 104.

5 Gustav Stickley, "Porches, Pergolas and Terraces: the charm of living out of doors," *Craftsman Homes*, Craftsman Publishing Company, New York, 1909, p. 97.

6 *The House*, Vol. 1, p. 105.

7 Ibid., p. 105.

8 Ibid., p. 105.

9 Voysey used caricature portraits in the construction of sundials, as fireplace and porch brackets, and in carved beam ends, but his clients were always included rather than ridiculed in the joke.

10 Phoebe Haydon, "The Memoirs of a Faithful Secretary" unpublished typescript, undated, p. 1. Papers in the possession of Felicity Ashbee and quoted in Alan Crawford, *C. R. Ashbee, architect, designer and romantic socialist*, Yale, London, 1895, p. 72.

11 Gustav Stickley, "Craftsman metal work," *Craftsman Homes*, p. 162.

12 Ibid., p. 164.

13 Clementina Black, *A new way of housekeeping*, W. Collins Sons & Co., London, 1918, p. 31.

14 Anon., "How to treat an ordinary hall," *The House*, Vol. 1, p. 104.

15 Ibid.

16 Ibid.

17 Although Charles Greene is not known to have been actively interested in theosophy before the publication of Claude Bragdon's *The Beautiful Necessity* in 1910, his earlier interests in Buddhism and transcendentalism may have informed the design of the Gamble House. See Travis Culwell, "D. L. James House Carmel, 1921, Building and Belief," *Style 1900*, Vol. 11, Number 1, 1997/8, p. 87.

18 *The House*, Vol. 1, p. 106, and H. C. Davidson, *The Book of the Home*, p. 119.

19 Hermann Muthesius, *The English House*, p. 205.

20 Rhoda and Agnes Garrett, "Suggestions for house decoration in painting, woodwork, and furniture," Macmillan & Co., London, 1876, p. 41.

21 M. H. Baillie Scott, *Houses and Gardens*, Newnes, London, 1906, p. 17.

22 Ibid., p. 17.

23 Ibid., p. 167.

24 Muthesius described this type of hall as "aping the large house" in *The English House*, p. 130. In addition to the six bedrooms for family and guests, there were two maids' rooms.

25 Ibid., p. 130 and p. 205.

26 Ibid., p. 90.

27 M. H. Baillie Scott, *Houses and Gardens*, p. 18.

28 M. H. Baillie Scott, "An Ideal Suburban House," *The Studio*, Vol. 3, 1894, p. 128.

29 For early photographs of the hall at Blackwell see figs. 105 and 321 in Hermann Muthesius, *The English House*, and p. 170 in Baillie Scott, *Houses and Gardens*.

30 M. H. Baillie Scott, *Houses and Gardens*, p. 18.

31 Ibid., p. 50.

32 The frieze is absent in the photograph of Blackwell published in Muthesius in 1904 but it is in place in a photograph of the hall published in Walter Shaw Sparrow (ed.), *The Modern Home*, Hodder and Stoughton, London, 1906. Not designed by Baillie Scott, it was selected from a catalog of patterns manufactured by Shand Kydd Ltd. See Diane Haigh, *Baillie Scott, The Artistic House*, Academy Editions, London, 1995, p. 29.

33 A reproduction of this interior perspective by Baillie Scott is published in black and white in *The Builder*, February 1900, Vol. 78, op. p. 190.

34 M. H. Baillie Scott, "A Country House," *The Studio*, Vol. 19, 1900, p. 30.

35 Ibid., p. 31.

36 Ibid., p. 32.

37 Hermann Muthesius, *The English House*, p. 205.

38 Ibid., p. 90.

39 C.F.A. Voysey, "Remarks on domestic entrance halls," *The Studio*, Vol. 21, 1901, p. 244.

Chapter Four

1 Margaret Oliphant, *Miss Marjoribanks*, Chatto & Windus, 1969 edition, p. 176. The novel was first published in serial form in *Blackwood's Magazine* in 1865–6, before the Arts and Crafts period, but the attitudes and the use of interiors which it describes continued beyond the close of the nineteenth century. Her account of Lucilla's "Evenings" is compatible with later descriptions of artistic salons in the novels of Shaw and James, and with Muthesius's 1904 account of English hospitality in *The English House*.

2 Margaret Oliphant, *Miss Marjoribanks*, p. 152.

3 Margaret Oliphant, *Miss Marjoribanks*, p. 109 and p. 121.

4 May Morris, *Collected Works*, Vol. 1, p. xxvi. Kate Faulkner painted tiles and, later, furniture for Morris & Co.

5 Anon., "The Story of Mary Augusta Huggins Gamble," unpublished typescript, p. 3, Box A, Folder II, Greene and Greene archives, Huntington Library, Los Angeles.

6 Hermann Muthesius, *The English House*, p. 216.

7 Ibid.

8 Ibid., p. 218.

9 John F. Runciman, "The Pianoforte: Past, Present, and Future," *Art Journal*, Vol. 46, 1894, p. 146. For a detailed analysis of the Arts and Crafts piano, see Ghenete Zelleke, "Harmonizing Form and Function: Mackay Hugh Baillie Scott and the Transformation of the Upright Piano," *The Art Institute of Chicago Museum Studies*, Vol. 19, No. 2, 1993, pp. 16–173.

10 Anon., "A Treasure Chest of Tone: A Departure in the Shape of the Upright Pianoforte," *The Artist*, Vol. 21, 1898, p. 65.

11 Ibid., p. 100.

12 Rhoda and Agnes Garrett, *Suggestions for house*

decoration in painting, woodwork, and furniture, Macmillan & Co., London 1876.

13 Philip Webb's site book, running on from a page dated 22 April 1895, records "pattern of Red for hall paneling." It is believed to have been painted white to make the hall lighter when Webb extended the room in 1898. I am grateful to Sheila Kirk and Arthur Grogan for this information.

14 Mrs. Joan Sherwood, *Manners and Social Usages,* Harper & Bros., New York, 1884, p. 22.

15 Ibid., p. 252.

16 Ibid.

17 Ibid., p. 247.

18 Hermann Muthesius, *The English House,* p. 70.

19 Mrs. Joan Sherwood, *Manners and Social Usages,* p. 248.

20 Henry James, *The Portrait of a Lady,* first published in 1881, Penguin Classics Edition, 1986, p. 438.

21 Henry James, *The Awkward Age,* first serialized in *Harper's Weekly* in 1899, Penguin Classics Edition, 1987, p. 89.

22 Hermann Muthesius, *The English House,* p. 215.

23 Voysey's kettle and stand was designed in 1893. It appears in his subsequent watercolor perspectives of complete interiors as a companion to his fire irons.

24 *The House,* Vol.1, p. 234.

25 The settle was usually set at right angles to the chimney breast in the drawing room so that the back of the piece as well as its front was intended to be viewed.

26 Hermann Muthesius, *The English House,* p. 212.

27 Margaret Oliphant, *Miss Marjoribanks,* p. 381.

28 Ibid.

29 Hermann Muthesius, *The English House,* p. 212.

30 Rhoda and Agnes Garrett, *Suggestions for house decoration,* p. 29.

31 *The House,* Vol. 6, 1899, p. 138.

32 Ibid.

33 Hermann Muthesius, *The English House,* p. 213. Henry James describes the crisp chintz and fresh flowers in his fictional drawing room at Plash in *A London Life,* (1936 edition), Charles Scribner's Sons, New York, p. 271.

34 Hermann Muthesius, *The English House,* p. 211.

35 Song lyrics by Corny Grain quoted in *The House,* Vol. 6, 1899, p. 138.

36 "Honesty" by George Frampton is illustrated in *The Studio* review of the 1896 Arts and Crafts Exhibition in London, Vol. 9, 1897, p. 117. It is still in place in Voysey's "Hill Close," Studland Bay, Dorset, designed in 1895–6.

37 W. R. Lethaby, "Ernest Gimson's London Days," Lethaby, Powell and Griggs, *Ernest Gimson, His Life and Work,* Shakespear Head Press, Stratford-upon-Avon, 1924, p. 5.

38 Ibid., p. 7.

39 Hermann Muthesius describes the process of making fibrous plaster panels in *The English House,* citing Baillie Scott's designs for Blackwell as an example, p. 175.

40 Letter from Philip Webb to James Beale, 20 January 1898, Standen Ms.176, West Sussex Record Office.

41 Although there is no documentary evidence to

suggest that the drawing room at Standen was closed in the winter, the exposed position of Melsetter and the size of the drawing room windows make it typical of Arts and Crafts houses in colder climates as a summer room only.

42 "Standen Memories," p. 13.

43 Morris & Co. produced embroidery patterns for genteel needleworkers and designed them as commissions for specific clients. Margaret Beale is known to have worked one of his finest early hangings, now in the Victoria & Albert Museum, in the 1870s before Standen was conceived, and the design for the drawing-room hanging "Artichoke" was originally commissioned by another of Webb's clients, Ada Goodman, for Smeaton Manor in Yorkshire. The "Artichoke" hangings are presently hung, for conservation reasons, in one of Standen's bedrooms but the National Trust hope to reinstate them in the drawing room.

44 I am grateful to Sheila Kirk, the authority on Philip Webb, for this information.

45 Although some of the furnishing of the drawing room at Standen is original, there are no inventories and very few early photographs of the interior. Many of the fine pieces in the room, including the Morris carpet, are a consequence of the inspired acquisition policy of Arthur and Helen Grogan in the 1970s.

46 Hermann Muthesius, *The English House,* p. 212.

47 Ibid., p. 216.

48 Letter from Philip Webb to Margaret Beale, 7 July 1894, West Sussex Record office, Standen Ms.174.

49 Ibid., Ms.174.

50 Anon., "The Artistic Development of the Extrolier," *The House,* Vol. 1, p. 23.

51 These sketches and notes in Charles Greene's hand are on small, unbound sheets of yellow note paper. Greene and Greene Project Records, Box 15, Series III, Environmental Design Library, The University of Berkeley, San Francisco.

52 Ibid., Box 15.

53 Mary Gamble's work book is in Box A, Folder I, Greene and Greene Archive, Huntington Library, Los Angeles.

54 Bertha M. Howland, "Reading Lamps Beautiful by Night and Day," *Indoors and Out,* Boston, Vol. 1, 1905.

55 The specifications for the Gamble House state that "Grueby or Rookwood tile" should be used, and it is thought that Grueby tiles decorate the living and dining room fireplaces while Rookwood tiles were probably used in Aunt Julia's bedroom. See Edward Bosley, *Gamble House,* Phaidon Press, London, 1992, no pagination, footnote 19.

56 See Rhoda and Agnes Garrett, *Suggestions for house decoration,* pp. 28–9 and Anon., "How to Furnish Tastefully for Five Hundred: The Drawing Room," *The House,* Vol. 6, 1899, p. 138.

57 See perspective watercolor published in *The Craftsman* in October 1905 and Gustav Stickley, "The Living Room: Its Many Uses and the Possibilities It Has for Comfort and Beauty," *Craftsman Homes,* pp. 129–137.

58 Charles Keeler, *The simple home,* P. Elder, San

Francisco, 1904, p. 31.

59 I am grateful to Dr. Robert Winter for this information about the Batchelder House, which is documented in the *Pasadena Daily News,* 19 February 1910.

60 In Voysey's designs the bird was a symbol for the spirit. See C.F.A. Voysey "Modern Symbolism," *The Architect & Contract Reporter,* Vol. 99, 15 February 1918, pp. 102–3.

61 Gussie Packard Dubois, "Progress Made on Plans for Art Hall," *Pasadena Star,* 23 November 1912.

62 Ibid., 23 November 1912.

63 Helena M. Sickert Swanwick, *I have been young,* quoted in Fiona MacCarthy, *William Morris, A Life for Our Time,* Faber and Faber Ltd., London, 1994, p. 399.

CHAPTER FIVE

1 Anon., "Be Agreeable at Meals," *The Ladies' Home Journal,* Vol. III, No. 2, San Francisco (not to be confused with the Philadelphia periodical), 1880, p. 10.

2 Ibid., p. 10.

3 In *Manners and Social Usages,* Mrs. Joan Sherwood devoted an entire chapter to "laying the dinner-table" as a subject for "painstaking thought, taste, and experience, and like all works of art, worthy of study." p. 265.

4 Flora Klickmann (ed.), *The Mistress of the Little House. What she should Know and what she should Do when She has an Untrained Servant,* The office of "The Girl's Own Paper & Woman's Magazine," London, 1919, p. 26.

5 Hermann Muthesius, *The English House,* p. 210.

6 Mrs. Joan Sherwood, *Manners and Social Usages,* p. 265.

7 See Hermann Muthesius, *The English House,* p. 210. There are archival photographs of the Beales arranging flowers.

8 Clementina Black, *A new way of housekeeping,* W. Collins Sons & Co., London, 1918.

9 Ibid., p. 5.

10 Mrs. Joan Sherwood, *Manners and Social Usages,* p. 262.

11 Ibid., p. 262.

12 "Standen Memories," p. 2. One of the Beale grandchildren however, Barton Worthington, recalled that it was he, rather than the butler, who announced the lady's appetite and that she was a famous poet of the period.

13 Hermann Muthesius, *The English House,* p. 207.

14 Anon., "On the Choice of Wall Papers. The decoration of the dining room," *The House,* Vol. 1, 1897, p. 78, and Hermann Muthesius, *The English House,* p. 210.

15 Hermann Muthesius, *The English House,* p. 206.

16 See Hermann Muthesius, *The English House,* p. 88, for a description of the fall in alcohol consumption.

17 M. H. Baillie Scott, "An Artist's House," *The Studio,* Vol. 9, 1896, p. 32.

18 Anon., "How to furnish tastefully for 'five hundred'. The dining room," *The House,* Vol. 5, 1899, p. 134.

19 Anon., "Sunny Rooms," *The Ladies' Home Journal,* San Francisco, Vol. 5, 1880, p. 14.

20 Rhoda and Agnes Garrett, *Suggestions for house*

decoration, p. 43.

21 Henry James writing about the Brigstocks in *The Spoils of Poynton*, first published in 1897, 1936 edition, Charles Scribner's Sons, New York, p. 7.

22 In a chapter on wood paneling, J. A. Gotch claimed that a room of nearly thirty feet by twenty feet could be panelled to a height of ten feet for fifty pounds and that the cost of paneling had been reduced by half in the last decade. Lawrence Weaver (ed.), *The House and its Equipment*, Country Life, London, 1918, p. 13.

23 Although as an exception to this rule the smoking room at Temple Disley, designed by Lutyens and published in Lawrence Weaver (ed.), *The House and its Equipment* (pp. 14–15) used unpainted deal paneling.

24 "Standen Memories," p. 14.

25 Arthur T. Bolton, "Wood chimney-pieces," Lawrence Weaver (ed.), *The House and its Equipment*, p. 33.

26 Letter from Philip Webb to Margaret Beale, 7 July 1894, Standen Ms. 174, West Sussex Record Office.

27 They now hang in the hall and billiard room respectively.

28 Anon., "The wife's secret," *The Ladies' Home Journal*, San Francisco, Vol. III, No. 2, 1888, p. 10.

29 Edward Bok, "The newspaper at breakfast," *The Ladies' Home Journal*, Vol. V, No. 1, 1895, p. 2.

30 "Standen Memories," p. 2.

31 Mary Lutyens, *To be Young*, Rupert Hart Davis, London, 1959, p. 14.

32 Letter from Edwin Lutyens to Lady Emily written in 1897, quoted in Christopher Hussey, *The Life of Sir Edwin Lutyens*, Country Life, London, 1953, pp. 64–7.

33 Ibid.

34 For a description of 29 Bloomsbury Square see Christopher Hussey, *The Life of Sir Edwin Lutyens*, p. 147.

35 Hermann Muthesius, *The English House*, p. 210.

36 May Morris, *Collected Works*, Vol. 1, p. xxvi.

37 D. S. MacColl, "The Arts and Crafts Exhibition," *Architectural Review*, Vol. 13, 1903, p. 187.

38 Hermann Muthesius, *The English House*, p. 196.

39 D. S. MacColl, "The Arts and Crafts Exhibition," *Architectural Review*, Vol. 13, 1903, p. 189.

40 Ibid., p. 187.

41 W. R. Lethaby, "Ernest Gimson's London Days," Lethaby, Powell & Griggs, *Ernest Gimson, His Life and Work*, Shakespear Head Press, Stratford-upon-Avon, 1924, p. 6.

42 Gimson and the Barnsleys moved to Ewen in 1893. After about a year they took workshops and living accommodation at Pinbury Park until the workshops moved to Daneway House, and they each built their own small houses nearby. Sidney Barnsley remained separate from the Daneway workshops, choosing to make furniture in a converted outbuilding next to his cottage.

43 For a detailed account of Gimson's rush-seated chairs see Annette Carruthers, *Ernest Gimson and the Cotswold group of craftsmen*, Leicestershire Museums, Leicester, 1978.

44 Gimson sold 20 copies of the rocking chair at the 1893 Arts and Crafts Exhibition. The price of £1 compared favorably with Benson table lamps which sold for £3 15s.

and with a much more elaborate and expensive inlaid sideboard designed by Blomfield which sold for £50. The sales accounts for the 1893 exhibition are in the National Archive of Art and Design in London, AAD 1/77–1980.

45 I am grateful to Neville Neal, who was trained by Edward Gardiner, for explaining the processes involved in making Gimson chairs to me. His workshop at Stockton near Rugby still makes the chairs in the traditional way.

46 Extract from the diaries of Dorothy Walker, 22 and 28 September 1899, published in Robin Tanner (ed.) *The Turn of the Century, extracts from the diaries of Dorothy Walker 1899, 1900, 1901*, The Old Stile Press, 1995, pp. 36–7. The following week the Barnsleys arrived in London for the Arts and Crafts Exhibition Society private view and Dorothy met them at the station and went shopping with them.

47 Quoted in Mary Comino, *Gimson and the Barnsleys, "Wonderful furniture of a commonplace kind,"* Evans Brothers Ltd., London, p. 133. Source of quote not identified, footnote missing.

48 C. R. Ashbee, quoted in Clive Aslett, "Rodmarton Manor, Glos. I and II," *Country Life*, Vol. 164, 19 October 1978, p. 1181.

49 See Annette Carruthers, *Ernest Gimson*, p. 8.

50 Arthur Oswald, "Rodmarton, Gloucestershire. The seat of the Hon. Claud Biddulph," *Country Life*, 4 April 1931, p. 427.

51 See C.F.A. Voysey, "Ideas in Things," T. Raffles Davison (editor), *The Arts connected with Building: Lectures on craftsmanship and design*, Batsford, London, 1909, p. 131.

52 Hermann Muthesius, *The English House*, p. 207.

53 Photographs of 37 Bidston Road, designed by Voysey for Mrs. Van Gruisen in 1902, were exhibited at the Arts and Crafts Exhibition of 1903 and published in *Dekorative Kunst* in 1902–3 and in *The Studio* in 1904.

54 Gustav Stickley, "Our native woods and the Craftsman method of finishing them," *Craftsman Homes*, p. 185.

55 Gustav Stickley, "The dining room as a center of hospitality and good cheer," *Craftsman Homes*, p. 140.

CHAPTER SIX

1 C.H.B. Quennell, "Kitchen and sculleries," Lawrence Weaver (ed.), *The House and its equipment*, p. 87.

2 *Cassell's Book of the Household*, Vol. 1, Cassell & Co. Ltd., London, 1889, p. 151.

3 Florence B. Jack (ed.), *The Woman's book, contains everything a woman ought to know'*, T. C. & E. C. Jack, London, 1911, p. 41.

4 *Cassell's Book of the Household*, Vol. 1, p. 152.

5 H. C. Davidson (ed.), *The Book of the Home*, Vol. 2, p. 171.

6 *Cassell's Book of the Household*, Vol. 1, p. 150.

7 *Cassell's Book of the Household*, Vol. 1, p. 328.

8 Ibid., p. 329.

9 Ibid.

10 Ibid.

11 H. C. Davidson, *The Book of the Home*, Vol. 2, p. 187.

12 *Cassell's Book of the Household*, Vol. 1, p. 150.

13 Ibid., Vol. 1, p. 329.

14 Ibid., p. 330.

15 Ibid., p. 176.

16 C.F.A. Voysey, "Ideas in Things," p. 125.

17 Ibid., p. 125.

18 Ibid.

19 Ibid., p. 126.

20 C.H.B. Quennell wrote that the kitchen and its offices were "in the same relation to the house as the heart ... to the body." Lawrence Weaver, *The House and its Equipment*, p. 87.

21 Webb is reputed to have done this at Standen, and Sheila Kirk believes that it would have been consistent with his practice if the cook had been with the family for a long time, but there is no known documentary evidence to support the anecdote.

22 C.H.B. Quennell, "Kitchens and Sculleries," Lawrence Weaver, *The House and its Equipment*, p. 90.

23 Ibid., p. 90.

24 H. C. Davidson, *The Book of the Home*, Vol. 3, p. 46.

25 Ibid., p. 171.

26 Ibid., p. 42.

27 C.H.B. Quennell, "Kitchens and Sculleries," p. 90.

28 For a summary of domestic refrigeration in 1912, see Dudley Gordon's chapter on "Refrigeration" in Lawrence Weaver, *The House and its Equipment*, pp. 93–96.

29 H. C. Davidson, *The Book of the Home*, Vol. 3, p. 60.

30 Hermann Muthesius, *The English House*, p. 100.

31 Anon., "Cooking and heating by electricity," *The House*, Vol. 1, p. 234.

32 Ibid.

33 Ibid.

34 Hermann Muthesius, *The English House*, p. 96.

35 Clementina Black, *A new way of housekeeping*, W. Collins Sons & Co., London, 1918, p. 34.

36 Hermann Muthesius, *The English House*, p. 98.

37 Esther Stone promotes and illustrates this type of efficient and hygienic kitchen in "The Modern Kitchen, Indoors and Out," Boston, Vol.1, 1905, pp. 218–302.

38 C.H.B. Quennell, "Kitchens and Sculleries," p. 89.

39 Gustav Stickley, "A convenient and well-equipped kitchen that simplifies the housework," *Craftsman Homes*, p. 142.

40 Charles Keeler, *The simple home*, P. Elder, San Francisco, 1904, p. 17.

41 Ibid., p. 53.

42 Ibid.

43 Ibid.

44 See John Ruskin, *Sesame and Lilies*, p. 87.

45 Gustav Stickley, "A convenient and well-equipped kitchen that simplifies the housework," *Craftsman Homes*, p. 143.

46 Charlotte Perkins Gilman, *The home, its work and influence*, William Heinemann, London, 1904, pp. 12–13.

47 Ibid., p. 261.

CHAPTER SEVEN

1 Hermann Muthesius, *The English House*, p. 92.

2 Ibid.

3 Edith Wharton, *The Age of Innocence*, p. 79.

4 Ibid.

5 H. C. Davidson (ed.), *The Book of the Home*, Vol. 1, p. 160.

6 Lady Barker, *The Bedroom and Boudoir*, Macmillan & Co., London, 1878, p. 1.

7 Hermann Muthesius, *The English House*, p. 224.

8 Flora Klickmann (ed.), *The Mistress of the Little House*, p. 20.

9 Flora Klickmann (ed.), *The Mistress of the Little House*, p. 19.

10 *The House*, Vol. 2, 1897, p. 87.

11 Hermann Muthesius, *The English House*, p. 194.

12 Penelope, "How to Furnish Tastefully for Five Hundred: the Spare Bedroom," *The House*, Vol. 5, 1899, p. 182.

13 Lady Barker, *The Bedroom and Boudoir*, p. 9.

14 Hermann Muthesius, *The English House*, p. 169.

15 *The House*, Vol. 5, 1899, p. 213.

16 C.F.A. Voysey, "Ideas in Things," p. 133.

17 Anon., "In search of 'the latest," *The House*, Vol. 1, 1897, p. 237. Voysey described the bed as the soul of the bedroom in "Ideas in Things," Op. cit. Heal's new range of wooden beds with iron lath frames are described in their catalog, *A consideration of the new wooden bed*, 1897, National Archive of Art and Design, AAD/1978/2/271.

18 Flora Klickmann, *The Mistress of the Little House*, p. 22.

19 Hermann Muthesius, *The English House*, p. 92.

20 Oliver Coleman, "Concerning bed rooms," *The House Beautiful*, Herbert Stone & Co., Chicago, Vol. 3, 1898, p. 23.

21 Penelope, "How to Furnish Tastefully for Five Hundred: the Spare Bedroom," *Art. cit.*, p. 182.

22 Letter from Philip Webb to Amy Beale, 23 August 1893, Standen Mss.169, West Sussex County Record Office.

23 C.H.B. Quennell, "Architectural Furniture," Lawrence Weaver (ed.), *The House and its Equipment*, p. 21.

24 *Cassell's Book of the Household*, Vol. 1, p. 179.

25 C.H.B. Quennell, "Fireplaces," Lawrence Weaver, *The House and its Equipment*, pp. 28–9.

26 Anon., "How to Furnish Tastefully for Five Hundred: the Best Bed-room and Dressing-room," *The House*, Vol. 5, 1899, p. 213.

27 I am grateful to Pamela Tudor-Craig for her astute observations on this subject.

28 *Cassell's Book of the Household*, p. 338.

29 Ibid.

30 Hermann Muthesius, *The English House*, p. 93.

31 *Cassell's Household Guide to Every Department of Practical Life*, Vol. 1, Cassell & Co., London, (no date given), p. 46.

32 C.H.B. Quennell, "The Bathroom," Lawrence Weaver (ed.), *The House and its Equipment*, p. 102.

33 Hermann Muthesius, *The English House*, p. 103.

34 Ibid., p. 102.

35 *Cassell's Book of the Household*, p. 340.

36 Hermann Muthesius, *The English House*, p. 93.

37 Ibid., p.237

38 Ibid., p.228

39 Edith Wharton, *The Age of Innocence*, p. 66.

40 Flora Klickmann, *The Mistress of the Little House*, p. 21.

41 Ibid., p. 22.

42 Oliver Coleman, "Concerning bed rooms," *The House Beautiful*, Vol. 3, 1898, p. 23.

43 Mrs. Glessner's dressing room could also be reached by a more circuitous route through her husband's dressing room and the bathroom.

44 *Cassell's Book of the Household*, Vol. 1, p. 181.

45 Ibid., p. 181.

46 Oliver Coleman, "Concerning bed rooms," *The House Beautiful*, Vol. 3, 1898, p. 19.

47 Ibid., p. 21.

48 Elizabeth Farwell, "Open-air Sleeping," *Sunset*, Vol. 8, 1909, p. 200.

49 Ibid., p. 203.

50 Ibid., p. 201.

51 Hermann Muthesius, *The English House*, pp. 224–5.

52 Greene and Greene Project Records, Box 15, Series III, Environmental Design Library, The University of Berkeley, San Francisco.

53 Hermann Muthesius, *The English House*, p. 231.

◼ SELECT BIBLIOGRAPHY ◼

Anscombe, Isabelle *Arts and Crafts Style* Phaidon Press, 1995

Ashbee, C. R. *A Book of Cottages and Little Houses* Batsford, 1906

Baillie Scott, M. H. *Houses and Gardens* George Newnes Ltd., 1906

Black, Clementina *A new way of housekeeping* W. Collins Sons & Co., 1918

Bosley, Edward *The Gamble House* Phaidon Press, 1992

Butler, A.S.G. *The Architecture of Sir Edwin Lutyens* Country Life, 1950

Carruthers, Annette *Ernest Gimson and the Cotswold group of craftsmen* Leicestershire Museums, 1978

Cassell's Book of the Household Cassell & Co. Ltd., 1889

Clark, Robert Judson *The Arts and Crafts Movement in America 1876–1916* Princeton University Press, 1972

Cobden-Sanderson, T. J. *The Arts and Crafts Movement* Hammersmith Publishing Society, 1905

Comino, Mary *Gimson and the Barnsleys, 'Wonderful furniture of a commonplace kind'* Evans Brothers Ltd., 1980

Cook, Clarence *The House Beautiful* Charles Scribner's Sons, 1881

Crawford, Alan *C. R. Ashbee: Architect, Designer & Romantic Socialist* Yale University Press, 1985

Cumming, Elizabeth and Wendy Kaplan *The Arts and Crafts Movement* Thames & Hudson, 1991

Davey, Peter *Arts and Crafts Architecture* Phaidon Press, 1995

Davidson, H. C. (ed.) *The Book of the Home. A Practical Guide to Household Management* The Gresham Publishing Co., 1904

Davison, Raffles T. *The Arts Connected with Building* Batsford, 1909

Elder-Duncan, J. H. *The House Beautiful and Useful* Cassell, 1911

Garnett, Oliver *Standen* The National Trust, 1993

Garnham, Trevor *Melsetter House* Phaidon Press, 1993

Garrett, Rhoda and Agnes, *Suggestions for house decoration in painting, woodwork, and furniture* Macmillan & Co., 1876

Gilman, Charlotte Perkins *The home, its work and influence* William Heinemann, 1904

Girouard, Mark *Life in the English Country House* Yale, 1978

Greensted, Mary *The Arts and Crafts Movement in the Cotswolds* Alan Sutton, 1993

Haigh, Diane *Baillie Scott: The Artistic House* Academy Editions, 1997

Harrington, Elaine *Henry Hobson Richardson, J. J. Glessner House, Chicago* Wasmuth, 1993

Haslam, Malcolm *Arts and Crafts Carpets* David Black, 1991

Haweis, Mrs. H. R. *The Art of Decoration* Chatto & Windus, 1881

Hitchmough, Wendy *Arts and Crafts Gardens* Pavilion, 1997

Hitchmough, Wendy *C.F.A. Voysey* Phaidon Press, 1995

Hussey, Christopher *The Life of Sir Edwin Lutyens* Country Life, 1953

Jekyll, Gertrude *Home and Garden* Longmans, 1900

Keeler, Charles Augustus *The Simple Home* P. Elder, 1904

Kaplan, Wendy (ed.) *"The Art that is Life": The Arts and Crafts Movement in America 1875–1920* Little, Brown & Co., 1987

Lethaby, Powell and Griggs *Ernest Gimson, His Life and Work* Shakespear Head Press, 1924

Lethaby, W. R *Philip Webb and his Work* Oxford University Press, 1935

Long, Helen *The Edwardian House* Manchester University Press, 1993

Makinson, Randell *Greene and Greene: Architecture as a Fine Art* Peregrine Smith, 1977

Massé, H.J.L.J. *The Art Workers' Guild 1884–1934* Shakespear Head Press, 1935

Morris, May *William Morris, Artist Writer Socialist* Basil Blackwell, 1935

Morris, May (ed.) *The Collected Works of William Morris* Longmans Green, 1910–15

Muthesius, Hermann *The English House* Crosby Lockwood Staples, 1979

Parker, Barry and Raymond Unwin *The Art of Building a*

Home Longmans Green, 1901

Parry, Linda *Textiles of the Arts and Crafts Movement* Thames & Hudson, 1988

Parry, Linda *William Morris* Philip Wilson, 1996

Quennell, M. & C.H.B. *A History of Everyday Things in England* Batsford, 1919

Rensselaer, Marianna Griswold *Henry Hobson Richardson and his works* Houghton Mifflin & Co., 1888

Sanders, Barry (ed.) *The Craftsman, An Anthology* Peregrine Smith, 1978

Service, Alistair *Edwardian Interiors* Barrie & Jenkins, 1982

Sherwood, Mrs. Joan *Manners and Social Usages*

Harper & Bros., 1884

Smith, Bruce *Greene & Greene: Master Builders of the American Arts and Crafts Movement* Thames & Hudson, 1998

Smith, Bruce and Yoshiko Yamamoto *The Beautiful Necessity: decorating with Arts and Crafts,* 1996

Stickley, Gustav *Craftsman Homes* Craftsman Publishing Co., 1909

Trapp, Kenneth (ed.) *The Arts and Crafts Movement in California. Living the Good Life* Abbeville Press, 1993

Weaver, Lawrence *Houses and Gardens by E. L. Lutyens* Country Life, 1913

Weaver, Lawrence *The House and its Equipment*

Country Life, 1912

Winter, Robert *American Bungalow Style* Simon and Schuster, 1996

Winter, Robert *The California Bungalow* Hennessey and Ingalls, 1980

Winter, Robert (ed.) *Toward a Simpler Way of Life* University of California Press, 1997

Woodbridge, Sally *Bernard Maybeck: Visionary Architect* Abbeville Press, 1992

▣ AUTHOR'S ACKNOWLEDGMENTS ▣

This book could not have been written without the support and practical help of many people. I would like to thank Colin Webb and Vivien James for proposing the title in the first place and for making it possible for me to research in America. Alan Crawford was extraordinarily generous on the numerous occasions when I asked for his advice and Ted Bosley arranged for me to stay at the Gamble House, a great honor, as well as sharing his considerable knowledge of Greene and Greene and the American Arts and Crafts Movement with me. I thank Bruce Smith and Yoshiko Yamamoto for their kindness and the valuable insights which they shared with me and I owe a special debt to Dr. Robert Winter for making my time in Pasadena so much fun. Randell Makinson, Robert Judson Clark, Bill Marquand, and Jim and Maxine Risley also helped to shape my understanding of the American Arts and Crafts Movement, Corina Carusi and Bernette Hoyt shared their knowledge of the Glessner House with me and I am grateful to Julie Reis, Kennan Miedema, Robert Kneisel, Vicki Laidig, Tawny Ryan Nelb, Barry Sears, Ann and

André Chaves, Jean and Roger Moss, and Siegfried Brockman.

I am privileged to have known the late John Brandon-Jones. Our meetings during the writing of this and my previous books were always a pleasure and his practical observations, his formidable memory and his sense of humor often set me straight and informed the theories that I had cooked up out of archive material. I thank Helen Brandon-Jones for her kindness and hospitality. I was fortunate to have met the late Elizabeth de Haas and I am especially grateful to Sheila Kirk for her generosity and magisterial authority in all matters relating to Philip Webb. I thank Ruth Gofton for her patience and enthusiasm over the representation of Standen, in words and photographs, and for reading the text with such care and insight. Martin Charles, as always, considered every aspect of the photography for the book and I am especially grateful to Elsie Seatter for her skill and hard work in creating an Arts and Crafts kitchen overnight.

I would like to thank Ruth Brown, Edward King, Michael and Wendy Max, Simon and Christine Biddulph, William and Fidelity Lancaster, Peyton Skipwith, Helen Castle, Frances Kelly and Dr. Maurice Howard. It has been a pleasure to work with Clare Johnson throughout the writing and editing of the text, and I am grateful to David Fordham for the care with which he has designed the book.

Finally, I thank my family: Dr. Sally Hitchmough was an expert and perceptive guide to nineteenth-century literature; Ken Baker and Grey and Matthew provided good diversions as well as quiet times for writing, and my parents, as always, were steadfast in their support. This book is dedicated to them.

▣ PICTURE ACKNOWLEDGMENTS ▣

Elizabeth Whiting & Associates: 10, 11, 73, 74, 77, 105, 107, 113, 157, 177, 178, 181

The Glessner House Museum, courtesy of Glessner House Museum, Chicago, Illinois: 61

Hedrich Blessing, Chicago, Illinois: 55, 57, 174

University Library, Cambridge: 21

V & A Museum Picture Library, London: 13, 14, 27, 108, 134

The majority of Arts and Crafts houses in Britain are in private ownership. They are not included in this list because they remain, primarily, family homes. Many fine Arts and Crafts elevations can be viewed from the street in towns and cities but country houses were generally designed with privacy as a priority. Their preservation depends upon the care and commitment of their owners and although some will welcome visitors who apply in writing in advance, explaining their interest, they are under no obligation to do so. Even the most generous owners would not relish the sight which one family found, early on a New Year's morning, of a tourist striding through their garden, camera at the ready.

BRITAIN

CUMBRIA

BRANTWOOD, Coniston
Although this is not an Arts and Crafts building it was John Ruskin's home from 1872.
Open daily all year
Tel. 01539 441396

BLACKWELL, Bowness-on-Windermere
M. H. Ballie Scott
1898
In the process of restoration as a center for Arts and Crafts to open in 2001
Tel. 01539 722464

DEVON

THE BARN, Fox Holes Hill, Exmouth
Edward Prior
1897
Country House Hotel
Tel. 01395 224411

CASTLE DROGO, Drewsteignton, nr. Exeter
Sir Edwin Lutyens
1910–30
National Trust
Open daily except Fridays, April to end October
Tel. 01647 433306

GLOUCESTERSHIRE

KELMSCOTT MANOR, nr. Lechlade
William Morris's country home and garden
1871–96
Owned by the Society of Antiquaries
Open every Wednesday, 11–1 and 2–5, and 3rd Saturday in each month 2–6. April to September
Thursday and Friday by appointment only
Tel. 01367 252486

OWLPEN MANOR, Uley, nr. Dursley
Tudor manor with important Arts and Crafts collections
Repaired by Norman Jewson 1925–6
Open Tuesday–Sunday and Bank Holiday Mondays, April to September
Tel. 01453 860261

RODMARTON MANOR, nr. Cirencester
Ernest Barnsley
1909–29
Open Wednesdays, Saturdays and Bank Holiday Mondays, 2–5, early May to end August
Groups at other times by appointment
Tel. 01285 841253

KENT

GREAT MAYTHAM HALL, Rolvenden
Sir Edwin Lutyens
1909
(Inspired *The Secret Garden* by Frances Hodgson Burnett)
House and garden open Wednesday and Thursday afternoons, May to September
Tel. 01580 241346

RED HOUSE, Red House Lane, Bexleyheath
William Morris and Philip Webb
1859
Open one weekend per month by prior arrangement
Telephone Edward Hollamby: 0181 303 8808

NORTHUMBERLAND

CRAGSIDE, Rothbury, Morpeth
R. Norman Shaw
1864–95
National Trust
Open Tuesday–Sunday and Bank Holiday Mondays, April to end October
Tel. 01669 620333

LINDISFARNE CASTLE, Holy Island, Berwick-upon-Tweed
Restored and converted by Sir Edwin Lutyens
1903
National Trust
Open Saturday–Thursday, April to end October
Tel. 01289 389244

SHROPSHIRE

ADCOTE SCHOOL, Little Ness, Shrewsbury
R. Norman Shaw
1879
Open late April to mid-October
Tel. 01939 260202

SURREY

GODDARDS, Abinger Lane, Abinger Common, Dorking
Sir Edwin Lutyens
1898–9
Available for bookings through the Landmark Trust
Tel. 01628 825925

MUNSTEAD WOOD, nr. Godalming
Sir Edwin Lutyens
From 1896
Open days to view the garden and the exterior of the house only, at end of April, end of May, and end of June, through the National Gardens Scheme

VANN, Hambledon
W. D. Caroe
1907–11
Open days to view the garden and the exterior of the house only, through the National Gardens Scheme, and private visits by arrangement
Telephone Mr & Mrs Caroe: 01428 683413

SUSSEX

GREAT DIXTER, Northiam
Additions by Sir Edwin Lutyens
From 1910
Open Tuesday–Sunday, all year
Tel. 01797 252878

LITTLE THAKEHAM, Merrywood Lane, Storrington
Sir Edwin Lutyens
1902
Country House Hotel
Tel. 01903 744416

STANDEN, nr. East Grinstead
Philip Webb
1891
National Trust
Open Wednesday–Sunday and Bank Holiday Mondays 12:30–4:30, late March to early November
Tel. 01342 323029

WEST MIDLANDS

WIGHTWICK MANOR, Wightwick Bank, nr. Wolverhampton
Edward Ould with Morris & Co. interiors
1887–93
National Trust
Open Thursday and Saturday, March to December
Tel. 01902 761108

SCOTLAND.

EAST LOTHIAN
GREY WALLS, Muirfield, Gullane
Sir Edwin Lutyens
1901
Country House Hotel
Tel. 01620 842144

FIFE
EARLSHALL, Leuchars
Restored by Sir Robert Lorimer
From 1892
Private visits by arrangement
Tel. 01334 839205

ORKNEY
MELSETTER, Island of Hoy
W. R. Lethaby
1898
Private visits by arrangement
Tel. 01856 791352

PERTHSHIRE
FORTINGALL
Most of this village, including cottages, school and hotel, designed as part of the Glenlyon House estate
James MacLaren
1889–90
In private ownership

STRATHCLYDE
THE HILL HOUSE, Upper Colquhoun Street, Helensburgh
C. R. Mackintosh and Margaret Macdonald Mackintosh
1902
National Trust for Scotland
Open daily 1:30–5:30, April to end October
Tel. 01436 67300

UNITED STATES

Neighborhoods and districts are open to visitors on public streets and sidewalks; most have no telephone contacts, Hotels are generally open year-round unless otherwise specified.

CALIFORNIA
CITY OF PASADENA
Bungalows big and small, from the Bungalow Heaven Historic District to essays in wood by Greene and Greene
Tel. (001) 626-585-2172.

GAMBLE HOUSE, 4 Westmoreland Place, Pasadena
Charles and Henry Greene
1909
The only Greene and Greene house—an "ultimate bungalow"—regularly open to the public
Open Thursday to Sunday.
Tel. 626-793-3334

MISSION INN, 3649 Mission Inn Avenue, Riverside
Arthur B. Benton, Myron E. Hunt, Elmer Grey, et al
1902–35
A delightfully eclectic landmark showing the style's Spanish mode
Guided tours daily
Tel. 909-781-8241

MARSTON HOUSE, 3525 Seventh Avenue, San Diego
Irving Gill
1904
Furnished with period objects and surrounded with an English garden; other Gill houses are down the street
Open Friday to Sunday
Tel. 619-298-3142

THE AHWAHNEE, Yosemite National Park
Gilbert Stanley Underwood
1927
A cliffside stone-and-wood lodge that still welcomes guests.
Guided tours year-round
Tel. 209-372-1407, 209-372-8441

DELAWARE
TOWN OF ARDEN, Six miles north of Wilmington
Will Price and Frank Stephens
Early 1900s to 1920s
A utopian community designed to attract artists and artisans, complete with a theater and guild hall

ILLINOIS
GLESSNER HOUSE, 1800 South Prairie Avenue, Chicago
H. H. Richardson
1887
A town house harboring a bedroom in the style of William Morris
Open Wednesday to Sunday
Tel. 312-326-1480

RAGDALE, 1260 North Green Bay Road, Lake Forest
Howard Van Doren Shaw
1896
A retreat for scholars and artists that was originally a summer cottage on fifty acres
Open Wednesday, June to September
Tel. 847-234-1063

FRANK LLOYD WRIGHT HOME AND STUDIO,
951 Chicago Avenue, Oak Park
Frank Lloyd Wright
1889–98
An inglenook, carved aphorisms, and furnishings revealing Wright's nod to Arts and Crafts ideals; many other Wright and Prairie School landmarks fill the neighborhood
Open daily
Tel. 708-848-1976

IOWA
ROCK CREST–ROCK GLEN, Along Willow Creek, Mason City
Walter Burley Griffin, Marion Mahoney, Barry Byrne, Frank Lloyd Wright, et al
1908–16

A picturesque community of Prairie-style houses exemplifying the era's planning principles

MICHIGAN
CRANBROOK HOUSE AND GARDENS, 380 Lone Pine Road, Bloomfield Hills
Albert Kahn
1908
A centerpiece of the Cranbrook educational community, set amid gardens and a lake
Open Thursday to Sunday, June to September
Tel. 248-645-3000

PEWABIC POTTERY, 10125 East Jefferson Avenue, Detroit
William B. Stratton
1907
The half-timbered cottage where Mary Chase Perry made pottery, now with a museum
Open Monday to Saturday
Tel. 313-822-0954

MINNESOTA
PURCELL–CUTTS HOUSE, 2328 Lake Place, Minneapolis
William Purcell and George Elmslie
1913
A Prairie-style gem whose coordinated interiors grew out of Arts and Crafts ideals
Open second weekend of the month
Tel. 612-870-3131

NEW JERSEY
CRAFTSMAN FARMS, 2352 Route 10 West at Manor Lane, Parsippany–Troy Hills
Gustav Stickley
1910
The log home built by the noted furniture maker as the center of a crafts community
Open Wednesday, Thursday, Saturday, and Sunday, April to October, and by appointment
Tel. 973-540-1165

NEW YORK
ROYCROFT COMMUNITY, Main and South Grove Streets, East Aurora
Elbert Hubbard
1894
A crafts campus modeled after William Morris's Kelmscott community of artisans
Open daily
Tel. 716-655-0571

STICKLEY MUSEUM, 300 Orchard Street, Fayeteville
Period furniture housed in the former Stickley factory
Open Tuesday
Tel. 315-682-5500

BYRDCLIFFE ART COLONY, Upper Byrdcliffe Road, Woodstock
Ralph Radcliffe Whitehead
1902

A small crafts commune founded to make furniture and art pottery
Guided tours Monday to Friday
Tel. 914-679-2079

NORTH CAROLINA
BILTMORE VILLAGE, Outside the Biltmore Estate, Asheville
Frederick Law Olmsted, Richard Morris Hunt, and Richard Sharp Smith
Late 1890s to 1910
A church, a depot, cottages, and half-timbered shops instigated by George Vanderbilt to serve his estate
Guided tours Monday to Saturday
Tel. 828-274-9707

GROVE PARK INN, 290 Macon Avenue, Asheville
Fred Seely
1913
A rustic stone resort that exudes the Arts and Crafts spirit from its roof to its Mission furnishings
Guided tours
Tel. 828-252-2711

OREGON
TIMBERLINE LODGE, Mount Hood National Forest
Gilbert Stanley Underwood
1937
A late but stellar example of the U.S. Government's rustic "Parkitecture" tradition
Guided tours Friday and Saturday
Tel. 503-272-3311

PENNSYLVANIA
FONTHILL AND MORAVIAN POTTERY AND TILE WORKS
Doylestown
Henry Chapman Mercer
1910–12
An eccentric castle and a still-working, Mission Revival factory built by an eccentric antiquarian
Open daily
Tel. 215-348-9461 (Fonthill); 215-345-6722 (Pottery)

VERMONT
NAULAKHA, Kipling Road, Dummerston
Henry Rutgers Marshall
1892
The shingled retreat where Rudyard Kipling, a friend of William Morris's, wrote two of his "Jungle" books
Available for rental stays
Tel. 802-254-6868

WYOMING
OLD FAITHFUL INN, Yellowstone National Park
Robert C. Reamer
1903
A world-famous hotel that is one of the largest log structures ever built
Open in summer
Tel. 307-344-7311

■ INDEX ■